Flavours of Home

Edited by Eileen Casey

Published in 2008 by Fiery Arrow Press

16, Watermeadow Park,

Old Bawn Tallaght,

Dublin 24

In Association with The Social Inclusion Unit,

South Dublin County Council.

ISBN 978-0-9552237-2-3

British Library Cataloguing in Publication Data. A CIP catalogue record for this book is available from the British Library

Cover painting by Rhyla Mae Santiago, Archbishop Ryan Senior National School, Balgaddy Road, Lucan, Co. Dublin.

Printed by Graph Print, Unit A9, Calmount Park, Ballymount, Dublin 12

Acknowledgements

Sincere gratitude to all who made *Flavours of Home* possible, particularly each and every contributor who so generously shared memories of family and home. Maria Finn, Senior Staff Officer with The Social Inclusion Unit is to be commended for her care and her attention to detail. Also, very much appreciated is the input of Krzysztof Podkonski and Sandra Hickey, The Social Inclusion Unit and the support of the staff of Lucan Library and Tallaght Library.

For their gracious response, special thanks to guest contributors Mr Conor Lenihan, Minister for Integration, Abdullahi Osama-El-Tom, Senior Lecturer of Anthropology at the National University of Ireland, Maynooth, Dr Declan Collinge, Writer and Academic, Lisburn-based Writer Lynda Tavakoli and Paris-based Artist Anne Cleary.

To Michael Finnegan, The Workers Party, who contributed to the success of the Lucan Workshop.

Thanks to all the schools in South Dublin who took part in the art competition. The support of teachers and students in this regard is very much appreciated. Congratulations to Rhyla Mae Santiago (aged 9) whose artwork is featured on the cover.

Quote from Brian Keenan's *An Evil Cradling*, published by Hutchinson, reprinted by permission of The Random House Group Ltd.

The organisation of the various workshops and this publication would not have been possible without the infrastructure and financial assistance of The Social Inclusion Unit, Community Services Department, South Dublin County Council.

Línte as Athair agus Mac 1966 (*Fearful Symmetry*, Mentor Books 1990)

Gan scáth gan eagla leanann Lennie air
In Iodáilis Bhaile Átha Cliath,
Fad a scagann Bean Uí Mhorelli
Sceallóga siosarnacha, a miongháire
Mantach chomh fairsing leis an Mezzogiorno, ag caochadh Súile faoin a chluain,
Á rá os íseal le m'athair 'Tá sé go breá Tá sé ar fónamh!'

Ar phlátaí gréisceacha
Fógraíonn cnámha bána an roic
Agus boladh na sceallóg
Teacht abhaile an athar agus an mhic...

Translation

...Undaunted, Lennie banters
In Dublin Italian
As Mrs Morelli drains
Sizzling chips, smiling
Gap-toothed, radiant
As the Mezzogiorno, winking
An eye under his spell,
Whispering to my father
'He's a very well
Keeping a very well!'

On greasy plates
The white-boned ribs of ray
And smell of chips
Tell of the return
Of father and son...

Contents

Introduction

Over the last few months it has been my pleasure to work with the contributors published here in *Flavours of Home*. Sincerest thanks are due to them for so generously sharing their individual stories. A huge debt of gratitude is owed to The Social Inclusion Unit, South Dublin County Council whose enthusiastic support has turned an idea into a multi-layered reality. Particular tribute is due to Maria Finn, Senior Staff Officer with the Social Inclusion Unit. Her energy and enthusiasm have been instrumental in ensuring that the process of gathering material for this publication, scheduling workshops and bringing together various organisational strands, progressed smoothly.

The contributors are drawn from diverse organisations and groups throughout South Dublin. These include; The Social Inclusion Unit, South Dublin Writing Groups; St. Muirin's (Tallaght), Virginia House (Tallaght), Clondalkin Writers (Clondalkin Adult Morning Education) and Lucan Writers (Lucan Library), together with Asylum Seekers and Ethnic Communities representing Somalia, New Zealand, Nigeria, France, The Democratic Republic of Congo, Poland, Russia and Catalonia. Also included are a number of previous contributors to 'Doors are for Opening' a Social Inclusion initiative which was held to celebrate International Day against Racism, 2008.

Special invitation was extended to Mr. Conor Lenihan, Minister for Integration, Abdullahi Osman El-Tom, Senior Lecturer of Anthropology at the National University of Ireland, Maynooth, Paris based artist Anne Cleary, currently working on In Context 3 (South Dublin County Council Per Cent Per Art Scheme) and Lisburn Writer Lynda Tavakoli. Lynda's contribution 'An Easy Crossing of the Cultural Divide' provides a valuable addition to the publication and also, her gift of tea leaves from Iran brought many smiles!

During the workshop process it was a privilege to hear so many heart-warming and insightful narratives, collected here for the first time, from so many different cultures and traditions. Each contributor has given so much so freely, painting colourful family portraits with vivid images and honest observations. 'Fiery Arrow', the imprint of *Flavours of Home* seems appropriate in light of the name being associated with St. Brigid, Patroness of Ireland and its warm welcome to the immigrant.

continued on next page

Flavours of Home, while providing recipes is first and foremost an album of family 'portraits' from around the world, written in the universal language that lies at the heart of every family. Some of the memories are unaccompanied by recipe, due to the nature of the story they tell. There are different variations in mood and tone throughout the collection, tales of grief and loss are side by side with lighter moments, a true reminder how shadow falls over family life, as surely as light. *Flavours of Home* is a collection to be read and reread, to be savoured and celebrated for the diversity of communities found between its pages but more importantly, for the similarities which exist between them. This publication also contains a journal facility whereby family memories and recipes can continue to be accessed and exchanged and most importantly, written down.

Eileen Casey

Roc agus Sceallóga/Ray and Chips

Declan Collinge

Is cuimhin liom, le linn dom a bheith i mo ghasúr, ag fás aníos i mBaile Bhailcín, ba beag an tóir ar a bhí ar iasc mar bhia. Dúradh linn go raibh sé 'go maith don inchinn' ach ba bheag aird a thugamar ar an gcomhairle seo. Faoin am sin, bhí an creideamh an-láidir agus níor itheadh feoil ar bith Dé hAoine. D'fhág sin go bhfacthas dúinn gur sórt píonóis an t-iasc agus b'fhearr linn fiú ubh a ithe ná é.

Aisteach mar scéal é, mar sin, gur tharraing roc agus sceallóga mé. Is cosúil go bhfaca mé m'athair agus mo sheanathair á ithe istoíche, go háirithe tar éis filleadh ó theach tábhairne an Cherry Tree tar éis cúpla pionta. Is ar éigean a bhí mé i mo shuí ag an am sin ach tá mé cinnte go bhfaca mé fuílleach an bhéile an mhaidin dar gcionn-na cnámha bána agus an fuidreamh orthu fós, an corr sceallóg fuar agus, go háirithe, an boladh blasta a mhair fós sa seomra bia.

As sin amach bhí mé sásta roc a ithe gach Aoine agus, ní hamháin sin, ach mar fhreastalaí páirt-aimseartha sa Cherry Tree agus mé im dhéagóir ag cur airgead i leataobh le haghaidh Honda 50 Cub, ba mhinic a bhuail mé isteach chuig Morelli's chun suipéar blasta a cheannach!

Cé go bhfuilimid uile níos sofaisticiúla ar na saolta seo agus taithí againn ar bhia agus ar fhíon den scoth, caithfidh mé a adhmháil go nithim roc agus sceallóga ó am go chéile agus go bhfaighim arís an blas súmhar sin a tharraing mé na blianta fada ó shin-cé go bhfuil praghas an éisc go scannallach anois!

Translation

I recall that, growing up in as a boy in Walkinstown, fish was not a popular meal. We were told that it was 'good for your brain' but we seldom heeded this advice. At that time religion was very strong and no meat was eaten on Friday. This meant that fish was seen as a sort of penance and we preferred to eat an egg instead.

Strangely enough, I was drawn to ray and chips. Perhaps it was because I'd seen my father and grandfather eating it at night especially after pints in The Cherry Tree. I was hardly up at that time but I'm sure I saw the remains of the meal the following morning- the white bones, still covered in batter, the odd cold chip and, of course, the delicious smell that lingered still in the dining room.

From then on I was happy to eat a ray every Friday and not only that, but as a part-time lounge boy in the Cherry Tree saving for a Honda 50 Cub, I often dropped into Morelli's to buy my tasty supper!

Although we're all so much more sophisticated nowadays, well-versed in top class food and wine, I have to admit that I still enjoy a ray and chips on occasion and I experience, once more, that succulent taste which enticed me all those years ago-though the price of fish today is scandalous!

Diving for Dinner

Patricia Devlin

I hear the seagull keen overhead. In the distance, I see silver black waves pout to kiss puffs of white cloud scudding across the horizon. The brightness of sunlight stings my eyes. I smell sea and taste its salt. My skin tingles to the buoyant brine. It's summer in New Zealand/Aotearoa on the coast, an hour before high tide; I am standing neck high in the waters of the estuary. Trish, my friend, companion in joys and sorrows, is a few feet away. We are laughing, bobbing up and down to the rhythm of the swell. "Look at our warriors", I say, gesturing towards the shore. On the beach, one is plugged into a sports broadcast, the other asleep under the shade of a newspaper collapsed over his face. Those mysterious partners of the male variety! Our husbands! Our children are playing close by them.

"See them guarding our ancestral coastline. Protecting our tribal progeny, watchful over us, their mates, willing to die, if necessary, to defend our honour while we gather kia moana", (Maori for 'food of the sea'), I expound to Trish. I am fantasying of course; comparing our quest for shellfish in the twenty-first century to the traditions of Maori hunters and gatherers, who peopled these shores for centuries before colonisation; the arrival of the European, the 'pakeha'.

"Yeah, right!" giggles Trish.

"I never thought of Anna", the red-headed six-year old, digging in the sand next to her father; as 'tribal progeny' but I suppose she is."

After a moment's reflection, Trish continues, "And who do you think is after our honour? Those two surfies leaning against the Volvo?" she jokes, pointing beyond the family tableau to the road where two bronzed, muscled-bound Greek Gods with surf boards, lean against a car. We splutter in laughter, as an unexpected wave breaks over our heads. We are imagining the prospect of our middle-aged husbands, armed with plastic buckets and spades challenging those Titans, who are intent on our undoing! We don't think!

All this time, we have been exploring the sandy bottom with our toes, twisting our hips from side to side in an exotic, underwater hula across the estuary dance floor. In this fashion, we search for mussels dislodged off rugged cliff-face rocks during storms, or heavy seas. These shellfish are carried in the surf until they are eventually deposited on incoming tides into the calms of the estuary. It's hard work to find a shoal of shellfish in these shallows. We've got about two hours to fill our 'kites' with enough mussels for dinner before the ebb of the tide is too powerful to swim against. A 'kite' is a Maori term for a collecting, or carrying bag. Trish is very traditional. She uses a woven, flax bag with handles, while I prefer a small, hessian sack.

Suddenly, Trish dives and comes up with a mussel: two black-purple coloured, elliptical shaped shells about five or six inches long, sealed together to protect the soft flesh of the sea creature inside. We mark the spot by visually aligning position in the water against some landmark, in this case, a gnarled, native shrub, flowering in bright red blossoms, a pohutakawa tree. Then we dive down again and again into the dark green water, our legs kicking hard against the pull of the tide to maintain our position over the treasure of the mussels. We pluck them quickly from the sand, hands full, and surface when our lungs burst gasping for air. At the surface we put the shells into the bags and dive yet again. Then exhausted, we take a break, in silence, afloat on the bouncing waves. The orange sun blazes in the western sky; the swell is rising and falling; we are timeless, divorced from gravity, cradled in Mother Ocean.

"Women in this place have fed their families like this for generations," I muse to Trish, breaking the spell. "Dive for dinner with a friend", she smiles back, "no better way to nurture da whanau (family) in a Kiwi way, CousieBro!", she lilts her intonation in Maori/English accent, and we laugh.

Preparing Raw Mussels (4 – 5 mussels for each person)

Gather mussels from the shore (never harvest near sewage or industrial plant out-falls (consult locals). To open, gently steam raw mussels in a little water until most shells have opened. Remove from heat immediately (over- heating will cause the mussel flesh to become rubbery). Rinse thoroughly in cold water to purge sand and set aside to cool.

To serve cold:

Soak overnight in a marinade of mild, white vinegar, (or white wine for adults) and chopped onions, enough to cover. Arrange the mussels (shelled or left in open shells) on a flat plate with a garnish of lettuce and or parsley. Strain the marinade and spoon a little over the mussels.

To serve warm:

Place the mussels (shelled or left in the shell) in an oven-proof dish. Lightly fry a clove of finely chopped garlic in about a quarter of a teaspoon of butter per mussel.

Add pepper, a little salt and chopped shallots or parsley. Drizzle over mussels and heat the dish in the oven until mussels are mouth-wateringly warm, do not over-cook.

Roast Beef with Trimmings

Mr Conor Lenihan, Minister for Integration

This is one of my favourite Sunday dinners. It never fails to remind me of long lunches at home when I was growing up. In the 1980's, like so many other people in Ireland, I had to move abroad to find work. I spent a few years working in London in a variety of jobs, including as a journalist and in Inner London Education Authority.

Although I loved the excitement of living in London, I always looked forward to the day when I would be able to return home for good. Whenever I came home for holidays, I would always ask my mother to make this dish.

Ingredients:

1 cut of beef - quantity depends on how much fat & bones is part of the cut you are buying

salt

pepper

1/2 a beef stock cube

1/2 an onion

one carrot

corn flour

one glass of white wine

one knob of butter

olive oil

Meat:

The meat should be left at room temperature for around one hour. Preheat your oven on gas mark 6, or 200 degrees centigrade (400 F). Cut about 40 grams off the meat for making the gravy. If you have beef stock this is not necessary. Rub salt and pepper into the beef. Put the roasting dish onto the hob and turn it on to high heat. Put enough olive to cover the bottom of the dish and wait until hot. Place the beef into the dish and lightly brown all sides. When browned place the dish into the preheated oven. After 10 minutes the heat can be reduced to gas mark 4.

I usually use around 1 Kilo of meat which takes around 50 -55 minutes.

Gravy:

Put one tblsp of cornflour into a glass and add some water and stir. Leave this aside.

Heat a small pot with some olive oil. Dice the 40 grams of beef you cut from your joint and add to the pot. Fry for about 3-4 minutes. Add a about half a finely chopped onion. Add a glass of wine, half a glass of water and one chopped carrot. You can now add half a beef stock cube for extra flavour and salt and pepper to taste. Reduce the heat and leave until about 5 minutes before your roast is ready. Using a colander, strain the stock into another pot. You can throw away the excess that is left behind in the colander.

Meat:

When your roast is ready, take it from the dish and place it on a wooden board and cover tightly with tin foil. It will need to sit for around 15 minutes.

Gravy:

Pour away the grease from the dish being careful to leave to meat juices in the dish. Then pour the stock into the meat juices in the roasting dish whilst heating it on the hob. Stir until all the bits dissolve. Pour your stock into the pot and leave on the heat. Again you need to be careful that there is no grease left in the stock. You can spoon this off the top if necessary. When your stock starts to boil slowly add the corn flour mixture in stages until you get the texture you require making sure it's not too thick. Finally add a nob of butter and stir until it melts through.

Serving:

When the fifteen minutes is up you can cut the meat into slices and serve with, roast and mashed potatoes, carrots, peas, savoy cabbage, roast parsnips, Yorkshire pudding and stuffing drizzled in homemade gravy.

An Easy Crossing of the Cultural Divide

Lynda Tavakoli

Allow me to invite you in. Come; unburden yourself of your dusty footwear and step into this modest apartment in Shahid Tehraniha Street where everything has been prepared for your arrival. Notice the intricacy of the pattern on the tablecloth spread out across the floor and the profusion of unusual dishes waiting to entice you, for this is where you will eat cross-legged in the traditional Persian way. Please don't be alarmed for there is no formality here and you will see that this mealtime is not so very different from home as you might think. The abundance of food – enough to feed a small army, says much about the importance of sharing and the gathering together of family be it in Iran or Ireland. So welcome to this Persian culinary adventure and enjoy with me one of your many choices - Chelow Khoresh Baadenjaan, a small flavour of my second home…

I have, of course, attempted to prepare this dish myself although admittedly never quite so well and never as authentically as my mother-in-law, as you might expect. So call this my 'Irish –Persian' recipe if you like and add to it some herbs and spices to your taste. I choose Chelow Khoresh Baadenjaan now because of its simplicity; the rice (*chelow*) included in the dish, for in Iran it is never the bridesmaid of the meal but always the bride. I love the sound of the sauce *Khoresh Baadenjan*, as though it must be something slightly naughty (that would be all the oil it soaks up in the frying!) or how the Farsi rolls from our English speaking tongue in that foreign and rather awkward way it does.

And so it has always been on my visits to Tehran – the easy crossing of a cultural divide with food a catalyst for the sharing of unconditional love and friendship with family and friends. I hope I have enticed you in to sample its pleasures for a short while at least. …. *Noushejân*!

Chelow Khoresh Baadenjaan is: A tang of lime lingering over your tongue, three kisses of welcome cheek to cheek, the haunting call for prayer through open windows, eating cross-legged on a Persian carpet, the love from family in a foreign land.

Chelow Khoresh Baadenjaan

Ingredients:

400 grams diced lamb or beef

8 small aubergines

3 medium onions

2 spoonfuls tomato paste

2 spoonfuls fresh lemon/lime juice

salt/black pepper

500 grams basmati rice

cooking oil

½ spoon of salt

Method:

Rice: (*Chelow*) Wash and soak in salted water for 3 hours. Drain. Two-thirds fill a non-stick pan with water and bring to boil. Add rice and salt and simmer until rice slightly softens. Drain. Pour a few spoonfuls of oil into empty pan and heap rice on top. Make a well in centre of rice (for steam to escape) and pour a few more spoonfuls of oil over the rice. Cover pan and cook over low heat for 30 minutes. This forms a crispy layer of rice (ta-dig) at the bottom of the pan when rice is cooked.

Sauce:(Khoresh Baadenjan) Fry thinly sliced onions until golden. Add meat and fry until colour changes. Bring 3 glasses of water to the boil and add to meat. Season and simmer over medium heat for one hour. Add tomato paste and lime/lemon juice. Cut aubergines into 1cm strips length-wise. Season and fry until golden and place over meat. Cover and cook on low heat for further 10 minutes.

Arrange rice on large flat dish with tad-ig on top and serve sauce on the side.

Courgette Soup

Anne Cleary

I invented this soup in the spring of 2006 in a desperate attempt to get some green vegetables into my twin daughters, then five years old. For the first five years of their lives Bo and Lotti refused any cooked vegetables that I offered them, while sustaining a deep attachment to a thick gooey concoction that came in square single-serving sachets, and was marked ' Babies first solid food'. Green Soup. They almost jumped for joy when they saw the cardboard packages come out of the cupboard, but dare I add a smidgen of fresh vegetables, or produce a soup any other colour than the statutory kaki green, the two little mouths took on a resolutely straight line, (Auntie Bidd, we always said) and the soup ended up in the bin.

I scanned the contents list on the packet many times, wondering what magic ingredient I was missing. My many attempts to simulate the original green soup were quickly unmasked and the pretender sent on its way.

Applying lateral thinking to the problem, I assessed the qualities of the ideal soup. Very smooth, no bits, very very mild, and green, above all the soup had to be green. What green vegetables are so mild as to be inoffensive to virtually everybody? The humble courgette of course, zucchini as our friends from across the Atlantic call it.

I prepared them well, I announced that I had discovered a recipe for the perfect green soup, that all children were known to adore this soup, that they were to be allowed to serve themselves with the fabulous soup ladle, and that anyway the new rule of the house was that they had to at least taste what is put before them.

Denis and I both held our breath as ladles of green soup splashed into bowls, onto the table, down fronts. Bo and Lotti picked up their spoons, squinting in simultaneous suspicion at the steaming green mess on the table before them.

Lotti tasted first, one spoon, pause, then another shorter pause, then several more in rapid succession. 'Can I have some more?' Bo was more sceptical. One taste, she put down her spoon and scowled. Everything all right? I asked casually. 'Hot' she muttered, but she ate three, then four spoons before pushing her plate away. Behind their backs I shot a triumphal glance at Denis, and did a small dance. Yes, I had won.

Courgette soup has become a staple part of our diet, and since then I have served it to many visiting children, all of whom have eaten it. They often ask for second helpings, as does Lotti every time I serve it, and one little girl even reminded her dad not to forget to get the recipe as they were saying goodbye.

We have tried the same soup on adults, and it seems to be equally appreciated, though one or two friends have suggested adding mint, chives, cream cheese etc. The blender variety is creamier and more suitable for children; the sieved version (which has bits in it) is more rustic and suitable to adult taste.

Courgette Soup

Ingredients: (for 4 people)

6/7 medium sized courgettes

generous knob of butter

1 clove of garlic

water

salt.

Method:

Wash the courgettes, top and tail them, and cut into chunks of approximately 1 inch. Melt the butter in a heavy bottomed pan, and sauté the courgettes slices with the garlic until they start to become slightly transparent. Add sufficient water to just cover the vegetables, and simmer for 20 minutes. Blend the vegetables with the cooking water in an electric blender or pass through a soup sieve. Add salt to taste (approximately ½ teaspoon for this quantity).

Glasgow Tattie Scones

Ann Marie Mullen

When my fridge was empty, except for a few potatoes, and all there was in my purse was dust and fluff, I would head for the kitchen and take out my old griddle. It looked a bit like a witch's cauldron except it had no sides. It was made of heavy black cast iron and the large handle shaped like a semi-circle had a little hook at the top to hang it above the coal fire on the boiler draw .

I would suspend it over my meager fire until it was good and hot and then I would grease it with a little lard. To test it was ready to cook on I would sprinkle a little flour on it and if the flour turned brown immediately then I knew it was ready for my scones.

The great thing about it having no sides was that you could watch the scones rise and lift them out easily with a fish slice. I would sit there in my little tenement flat warming myself by the fire and breathing in their fluffy odour. When they were cooked I would spread some butter over them and gobble them down till my belly was warm and full. Heavenly warmth for all the senses.

Here's a simple recipe for the next time you find yourself with just potatoes and you want a treat. Don't worry about the griddle, a frying pan does the job too.

Potato Scones

Ingredients:

1/2 lb cooked potatoes

2 oz flour

1/2 oz butter

Pinch of salt

A little milk or buttermilk to bind

Method:

Grease a griddle or heavy frying pan. Mash the potatoes with butter and a little milk and mix with a spoon. Add the salt and a little of the flour. Use your fingers to knead the mixture, adding more flour until it is all taken up and the dough is fairly stiff. Turn out on to a floured surface. Roll out to 1/4 inch thick and cut into rounds using a cup as a cutter. Place on the hot greased griddle or frying-pan. Cook for about 2 minutes until the underside is brown. Turn and repeat on the other side. Serve piping hot, spread with butter, or with a hot fried egg on top for a little luxury. Yummy!

The Cucumber Season

Maria Petrovicheva McManus

I am from Vnukova (Moscow green zone). It is surrounded by lakes and forests. Vnukoa airport is nearby and about 30 minutes bus journey to the city centre. All my family have a connection with the airport – my granddad was a pilot during the Second World War (a survivor) and he was granted the status of 'war hero'. My dad was a pilot in the past and now both of my parents are air traffic controllers. I have one brother. In fact I am the only girl in the family, as all my first cousins are boys.

I remember that one time when my mom, myself and my brother were going away for a holiday for two weeks. My father and my cat were the only ones staying at home. It was the end of august and it was 'cucumber season' in Russia (I come from a family that grew most of its own vegetables). There were enough vegetables for four people for a whole year. However, cucumbers will go to waste if they left on the ground for too long, so my dad and my cat were left with a challenge – to eat as many cucumbers as they could for those two weeks that we were going to be away. I should point out as well that my dad doesn't cook at all! So all that they had to eat was cucumbers for breakfast, cucumbers for lunch and...yes, you've guessed it, cucumbers for dinner!

After a few days of this strict diet, my dad discovered the kitchen, an oven and apples and flour. He put these few ingredients together (all from his own childhood memories) to make an apple pie. The cat was getting a share of the meal. So, after a week of this food my lazy household cat went to the forests nearby. After a few days of training he managed to capture small birds and other small animals who lived in the forest. And my dad was getting a fair share of those meals as well!. My cat would bring an odd bird or mouse to the house, leave it on the floor in front of my dad as if saying "Here Master, this is how meat looks, it is good for you, go ahead and have some.."

After we came back from the holidays, we found our cat in top physical condition and we found out the forgotten recipe from my dad's childhood – an apple pie!

Apple Pie (enough for 4 people)

Ingredients:

1kg green apples

1 cup of plain flour

1 cup of sugar

3 eggs

butter and dry bread crumbs for the base

Method:

Wash apples, take out the centre and cut them into small (bite-sized) pieces. Grease the round base of a baking tin with butter and sprinkle it with bread crumbs. Put apples loose into the base. Mix eggs, sugar and flour together in a bowl and pour it over the apples. Put into a pre-heated oven and then make yourself a cup of tea – the pie will be ready in 20-30 minutes. To check if it is ready, just put a wooden match in and out (straight away) of the centre of the pastry and if the match is dry – your pie is ready.

This pie is very easy to make and should help in getting rid of that 'can't cook' problem!

Aromas from The Republic

Jim Archer

The fire blazed half-way up the chimney; in the corner the new Bush wireless with the spectacular green eye played colourless piano music.

"I'm sick of that bloody stuff on Radio Eireann" said my uncle.

"Whatever happened to the old opera……. 'Maritana' ……. now there's music for ye". His eyes brightened.

"Did you know that Cork City was famous the world over for its love and knowledge of opera?" I nodded my head.   My uncle - a small rotund man with a cigarette voice and a heart as big as Africa was holding centre stage in the tiny kitchen. Behind him my aunt worked feverishly – the New World gas stove rising to the occasion as the smell of steak and onions filled the kitchen and began to stalk our noses. My nose was young – just seven. My grandfather and grandmother had very old noses.

"Johnny always loved steak and onions" my aunt muttered into the stove. He was back home in Cork from Birmingham having lived through the war as a bomb-damage worker. And he was now home for good.

As the aromas from the noisy pan tantalised my nose even more I began to think that like my uncle I could get to like steak and onions myself. In the half-light on a grey November day everything was bubbling up nicely – boiling water was gently poured on to the chump steak and onions and allowed to sizzle; next a cup of Bisto, all brown and creamy was added to the pan followed by a fistful of fresh herbs. The sprig of thyme held a special position and was added to the pan all by itself. The whole ritual was finished off with a generous sprinkling of salt and black pepper. The dollop of Colman's mustard completed the proceedings. All were allowed to settle down and gently simmer.

The spuds bursting from their overcoats were spilled onto the large blue Queen Victoria plate and placed on the table in front of the fire. By now the gravy was reducing and this resulted in sending even more intense aromas coasting round the kitchen and sending my senses into fever pitch heights. I pulled my seat up next to my uncle as my aunt laid out the plate before us. The fresh *Simcox* loaf (the name of the company before *Mother's Pride* took it over, to the very best of my memory) was sent along to mop up the gravy. Heaven – no, Heaven on earth is the way I remember that taste.

My grandfather and my grandmother dozing on their chairs, the fire licking the chimney, my aunt's bib with the one string forever falling down, and my uncle home in Cork for good and me a 'garsun' of seven tasting steak for the very first time.

Chump Steak and Onions

with large flowery potatoes and hot fresh thick loaf (Cork City Style)

Method:

Fry chump steak until tender. Cut large onion in rings and add to pan and brown. Add boiling water to pan. Add a strong cup of Bisto and fresh herbs. Add thyme, a dollop of Colman's mustard, salt and black pepper. Allow to simmer. Boil a pot of flowery large spuds in their jackets. Serve with fresh thick loaf.

Suji Ka Halwa

Leyla Abdi

This is my memory. When I was growing up I liked to cook food. I remember I said to my mom "you have to teach me how to cook" and she try to teach me Halwa.

Halwa is sweet, it's some kind of sweet dish and we like to eat it when we have a party or a wedding and now I can cook it. It also reminds me of that special time with my mother.

Suji Ka Halwa (Semolina Pudding)

Ingredients:

1 cup suji (semolina)

¾ cup sugar

1.5 cup whole milk

1.5 cup water

3 tbsp ghee, butter or margarine

½ tsp cardamom (Elaichi)

2tbsp raisin

Garnish:

2 tbsp raisin

2 tbsp cashew nuts

Preparation:

Heat ghee, butter or margarine in a wok. Add cardamom and heat a few seconds in medium heat. Add semolina and heat for a few minutes with constant stirring in low-medium heat. Add sugar and half of both raisin and cashew. Heat for a few more minutes in low-medium heat. Add water and milk. Mix well and heat until you get desired consistency (usually somewhat like watery dough or thick pudding). Garnish with remaining raisin and cashew nuts. Serve either hot (preferred) or cold.

Flavours of Home

Family Memory

_____

_____

_____

_____

_____

_____

_____

_____

_____

_____

_____

_____

_____

A Bowl of Ambrosia

Aine Lyons

Our family had no store of recipes. There was no history of passing on the secret of a Christmas pudding, steamed in a muslin cloth and hung on the back of the kitchen door ready for the big day. We learned by watching and waiting, usually with the taste of hunger flavouring every dish that Mam produced. These were the war years, the nineteen forties, everything was scarce or rationed and ingredients hard to come by.

When we got older, and the war ended, food became more plentiful. Friday was fish day and at that time, fish was cheap. Our favourite was smoked cod, cooked in white sauce and onions. I have cooked that food lots of times for my own family and while they love it, to me it could never taste the same as on those Fridays long ago. Looking back with fresh eyes, I realise many of the dishes were associated with the time of the year. Mam would save in a Christmas club, so much money per week over a number of weeks. There was great excitement when Dad would carry in the turkey.

The high point of the week was the big fry-up on Saturday evenings. When Mam came home from town we could get the Hafner smell before it hit the pan. It seemed like all of Dublin had sausages, rashers, and pudding, because the smell appeared to run down the street like it had legs. Maybe because we had to go to Mass and Holy Communion on Sunday morning, and we got no breakfast till we came home, that made that meal so special. We lived in a small village called Milltown on the outskirts of the city. Our small house was only a few doors away from my paternal grandparents who were country people, from Meath and Wicklow. They had a yard full of hens, pigs and assorted other animals like our pet donkey. In the big field behind the house they grew vegetables, and all different kinds of fruit. This small-holding was how they survived. They kept an ass and cart for collecting waste food. Grandfather had a 'round' and on that round he collected the waste food people kept for him and he also sold them fresh eggs and vegetables.

In terms of what we like to think of today as organic food, well my grandparents were Green with a capital letter. They got up early to feed the animals and I, being their eldest grandchild, 'granny grey' as everyone called me, was always there to feed the chickens. About twelve o'clock we had dinner. Every day it was the same, a large bowl of steaming potatoes, fresh cabbage with big white hearts, a rasher, and if things were good, a knob of butter. A feast fit for a king, all straight from the garden, except the rasher of course. "Balls of flour" Grandfather would say in a satisfied voice and he was right.

Now and again, especially when we had visitors, we would have a special Sunday tea when the mouth-watering smell of apple dumpling greeted us as we came in from playing skipping or piggy beds. I'd travel a long way now for that special meal, but sometimes memories are better than recipes.

Now we are grandparents, our children, with their children, visit us on Saturdays. The grandchildren love the special vegetable soup that Grandfather makes, and he teases them about the recipe. I wonder when they have children will they look back with pleasure at the memory of Saturday and that soup?

Risotto for Friendship

Nadine Carole Ditchou

I choose risotto because it reminds me of my family I left in my country, The Democratic Republic of Congo. It reminds me also of my childhood and especially my late Grandmother. When my parents died in 1999 I was fifteen years old and I had to live with Grandmother. We were not rich at all but with this food we would not sleep with empty bellies and with it we could be happy. It was not expensive and we loved the taste. Even if we had to eat the same food every day we would not complain because despite the fact that it was almost all we could afford, it was also something we liked. And the fact that it does not take long to cook was also a good point. After a long day spent working on the farm or in the market to sell things we would not have the patience to wait for more than thirty minutes to eat!

I am very happy Grandmother taught me to cook this dish because I can teach my friends how to do it too.

Risotto: (fried rice with spicy tomatoes and beef meat)

Ingredients:

rice

tomatoes

onions

spring onions

peppers, yellow, green and red.

white pepper

carrot

parsley

cube of chicken stock

salt

beef meat (boiled for 10 minutes)

vegetable oil

Method:

Fry the onions and spring onions in the hot vegetable oil, add carrots, pepper, parsley. After 7 minutes add tomatoes and the beef meat with the water it was boiled in. When it is boiling, add the rice, add water progressively until the rice is cooked. Then let the water dry completely and it is ready to serve.

Tramlines

Marie Morris

I used to visit my granny who lived in a very small cottage in Terenure, Dublin, (No. 6 Tramway Cottages to be precise - so called because all the cottages on the road were lived in by tram drivers and their families). I was always amazed at how many loaves of brown bread she could produce from her tiny scullery. She would always give me a drink of lemonade and a slice of her brown bread generously covered with her home-made blackberry jam. It was gorgeous. The blackberries were picked by us from the bushes on the Greenhill's Road - when it was all countryside and not built-up like today. When my grandfather came home after driving the trams he would sit at the table pouring his tea from a big mug onto a saucer and carefully lift it and sip away which I thought was very funny. This was because he couldn't wait for the tea to cool down.

My granny always wore a big apron which was covered in flour and there was a big pocket in the front. When I'd be leaving with my mam she always pulled a three-penny bit from her pocket to give to me. And sometimes she used to put money in the brown bread. That's why all my brothers and sisters loved eating her brown bread because of the excitement of finding money in it. Even today one of my favourite snacks with a cuppa is a thick slice of home-made brown bread with home- made jam and there is always a loaf of brown bread in the bread bin in our house. When I am eating home- made brown bread I can almost see my granny's smiling face looking over me and I hear her voice saying " I bet you won't find any money in that slice of bread!"

Home-Made Brown Bread

Ingredients:

8 oz brown wholemeal flour

8 oz plain flour

1 tsp baking powder

1 tsp bread soda

1 tsp salt

1 egg

2 large cups of buttermilk. (12 oz liquid)

Method:

Sieve all the dry ingredients into a large bowl. Make a hole in the middle and pour in the liquid mixture and the beaten egg. Mix together until a soft dough has formed. Turn out on a floured board and knead lightly. Then transfer into the greased loaf tin and bake in the oven for 30 minutes at 425 degrees and then reduce to 350 degrees for another 40 minutes. When baked, cool slightly in tin before turning onto wire tray to finish cooling.

Once Upon a Shepherd's Pie Day

Dee Kelly

School was less than fifteen minutes walk away from home which meant myself, two sisters and two brothers came home to dinner in the middle of the school day. Walking home was safe, as you were never alone, other school children, some younger, some older all heading the same direction, one by one going into their homes. Growing up in the early 1970's the way home from school was safe, Terenure was safe, Dublin was safe. We knew most of the people who lived along the street with the lovely Cherry Blossom trees, and they knew us also. These older people always seemed to be busy gardening, sweeping their driveways, washing windows, putting out the bins, chatting to their neighbours, all part of their day's work.

There was nothing better than arriving into the kitchen to the warming smell of my mother's shepherd's pie, on a cold wet day. The big kitchen table was already set for us to burst in the door. The red plastic radio with one big shiny dial on the front would be on, with the one o'clock news, not that I had any interest in the news, or anything that happened outside my life of home and school. The radio was my mother's contact to the world outside of her spotlessly clean kitchen and endless cooking and housework. Unlike nowadays there was no TV in the kitchen; the only TV in the house was in the sitting room which would only be turned on after school.

On one particular day I felt a bit nervous opening the kitchen door at dinner time. What would Mammy say when she saw my black eye. Would she believe that it was a complete accident that my face connected with someone else's foot in gym class? I hated gym class which was held indoors, I much preferred getting out in the fresh air to play hockey or netball, even if it was raining. As I tried to explain how I ended up with the black eye, Mammy put a plate of shepherd's pie on the table in front of me. The shepherd's pie was hot but not too hot that you would burn your mouth. It had a warming beefy smell not spicy like a curry and the mashed potato topping was baked to perfection. Mammy liked making shepherd's pie as the whole family would eat it, some days she would have prepared several dinners to suit the fussy eaters, my mother could have run a posh restaurant in Dublin with such management skills. Lasagna, pizza and other convenience foods were unheard of in our house in the early 1970's. Italy was the country shaped like a big boot in my school atlas and Rome was where the Pope lived.

But back to this particular day. As I was tucking into my dinner I heard my mother at the bottom of the stair calling "Come down quick and see Deirdre's black eye, quick before she goes back to school". A few minutes later, down the stairs comes a reluctant but curious younger sister who was on a "I've got a pain in my tummy" day off school. Not overly impressed with my black eye but before my younger sister could retreat back up to her sick bed she was told to sit at the table with everyone else and it was not long until she had eaten a plate of shepherd's pie. There was no fooling my mother about being sick, as you only got meals in bed and a comic from the shop if you were really sick. I think my black eye saved my mother an extra trip up and down the stairs that day.

Too hungry to talk the dinner was devoured quickly and it wasn't long before school books were opened. It was a race against the clock to complete last minute homework. Coats and shoes dried from the heat in the kitchen, we all went back to school for the afternoon, happy after seeing Mammy and having a lovely hot meal. The other school children who stayed in school for lunch would have only had sandwiches and a cold drink. Thinking back now wasn't it terrible to leave Mammy alone with all the washing and cleaning up as my family had no dish washing machine back then?

Shepherd's Pie

Ingredients:

1 oz margarine

1 large onion

1 oz plain flour

½ pt beef stock

1 pound mince beef

1 tbsp tomato puree

salt & pepper

Topping:

1 pound cooked potatoes

1 oz margarine

2 tbsp milk

salt & pepper

Method:

Melt margarine and fry onion over a low heat. Add flour and stir until beginning to brown, again over a low heat. Stir in beef stock, add remaining ingredients. Bring to boil, cover and simmer gently for 30 minutes. Pour into a one and a half pint dish. For topping, mash potatoes with margarine, milk and seasoning. Spread over meat. Place under grill for five minutes until brown or bake in oven (375F, Gas 5) for 15 to 20 minutes. Serve with green vegetables or carrots.

Six for breakfast

Maria Wallace Mir

I was born in an idyllic place called Platja d'Aro at a time when the name of that hamlet was never allowed to exist in its native Catalan, but had always to be written in Castilian, or Spanish, as Playa de Aro. My parents were farmers, like most people living then in that rugged coastline that later became known as the Costa Brava. We lived on a hillside overlooking songs of light and colour rising from the valley and the sea.

It's nine thirty in the morning, and as expected in Sant Feliu de Guíxols, a seaside town a stone's throw south from were I was born, it's sunny and already very warm. I'm meeting friends in *L'Aroma*, a vaulted-ceiling café in the market square. Being the last day of my holiday, this is a farewell breakfast reunion.

Six cups of dark and thick, melted and steaming chocolate are placed on the table, and a mountain of toasted, three-inch long fingers of bread, is left on a large plate in the centre.

We start dipping toast fingers into the sweet darkness of the chocolate remembering that during our childhood we had such a feast only on very exceptional occasions. We relish each bread dipping, the chocolate so thick the stick-like fingers can stand in the centre of the cup, still, as a sentinel would. Its bitter-sweetness, its velvety feel on the tongue and the crunchiness of the toast invariably elicits spontaneous and long ooohs and aaahs.

The conversation veers to the ever-welcomed yearly fete, which would go on for days, and when stands, stalls and funfair carousels transformed the quiet places we lived in. The fairs were a release from the unrelenting harsh-working days of the peasant, and somehow akin to the carnivalesque tradition of centuries ago.

My new white shoes feel odd, nice but odd. I can't wriggle my toes in them. I like the orange dotted cream dress, but father says it looks too big on me. "Soon enough it won't", mother replies. I grip her hand, tightly. High pitched sounds are explosions in my ears accustomed to the faint breathing from wheat and barley fields, to conversations twittered between trees, to wind murmurs and sea monologues. Amid the incomprehension of vendors' loud calls, the laughter and the crackling from old gramophones, the unmistakable happy tune of the merry-go-round. I gallop round and round, and happy, into the land of every bedtime fairytale.

Our six cups are empty. We've travelled miles into the past, a place of sunshine and innocence. Outside, the sun is still shining, stronger then ever, and innocently we trust that there will be many other breakfast gatherings as this one.

A Tale of Two Sons

Omolola Alorge

I have two sons. Festos is three and a half years old and he was born on 9th August, 2004. He does not eat a lot. He selects what he will eat and won't eat except you force him but at the end he will tell you that he does not want the food.

He is a good boy. He likes to play with other kids around him and he is kind and lovely and also friendly. We live in Killinarden, Tallaght.

Goodluck is ten and a half months. He eats everything that comes to his mouth. He does not select. He is a good boy and he also likes to play.

 I love my two sons Festos and Goodluck.

Soap Soup

Bridget Connors

I come from a family of seven children, three girls and four boys. I am the second youngest. We used to live in Captain's Road, Crumlin in Dublin. I have very fond memories of that house. We played in the back garden a lot. Dad made a swing out of an old bed. It had a big chain on it and a wooden seat. He was always working nights so we would go to bed early and Mum would tell us stories of her younger days. Other times, me and my friends would dress up with lace curtains, pretending to be brides getting married.

I remember the big table we had in the sitting-room cum kitchen and we had many happy mealtimes around that table. After our meal, Mum would put the big teapot on that table and we would all get a cup of tea. As there were never enough cups, some would drink out of jam-jars with no sugar. We only got sugar at the weekend. The rest was put away for Dad's tea. We were so happy sitting there as a family, the old-fashioned wood encased radio playing in the back-ground. I remember the station that was on, 'music while you work'. We had no television in those days or fridges either. I can still see the milk in a bucket of water to keep it fresh. When the table was cleared and the homework started around the table, we would hear the door open and Dad coming in with his push-bike. Sometimes he would bring in stuff he had found on a skip. Toys or wood. He was a man who always looked in skips, he always said that one man's rubbish is another man's treasure.

He would bring the wood out the back and my older brothers would cut it into sticks they would then wrap into a neat bundle. They would fill up an old pram (it was very deep) with all these bundles and sell them. They knocked at all the doors on the street just to get a few bob for my mum. Around 1967, my dad was minding the seven of us children. My mum was in hospital having another child. None of us ever thought my dad could boil as much as water. We never saw him at the cooker. I was watching his every move as he cooked our dinner. We did not know what to expect. He boiled a pot of potatoes, then he got a ring of white pudding, cut it up and put it on the pan with some fried onions. The smell was lovely. When the potatoes were cooked, he mashed them with a milk bottle. I remember that well as I was frightened the bottle would break and go into our dinner. Then, he put the pudding and onions into the mashed potatoes and added pepper. It was lovely on the bread. All of us children were so amazed at the thoughts of my dad making our dinner. Then later that night I saw him getting stale bread and putting it into a basin with a little water. Next day he put in some raisins and an egg and milk and put it in a big tin and baked it in the oven. That was called bread pudding. We loved it and we all said we hoped Mum would go away again so my dad could do the cooking. Back then, nothing went to waste, even stale bread was recycled. However, there was a particular incident which resulted in waste.

Mum used to make our favourite dinner, coddle, on Mondays and Saturdays. Coming in from school on Mondays the smell would hit us the minute we walked in the door. First, Mum would put a big pot on the cooker filled with water. Then, she'd add sausages, rashers, carrots, onions and as we used to say in the early sixties, "half a stone of potatoes". Then a packet of oxtail soup. When it came to the boil she would add parsley and thyme and she would let it simmer for two hours. The smell went around the house. It was lovely.

I remember my brothers and sisters getting bread when Mum was not looking and dipping the bread into the soup – before running up the stairs so Mum would not see them burning their fingers. I was too small then to see into the pot but if I stood on a chair I could see that the pot was full up to the brim. I will always remember the time my mum was in such a hurry one day, washing the potatoes at the sink before throwing them into the soup. A while later she could not understand why there were suds in the coddle. She looked around and then realised she had put the bar of carbolic soap (used for washing clothes) in as well. The big pot of coddle was thrown out to the dogs. They did not mind the soap but God only knows what we had for dinner that day.

Soap Soup

Ingredients:

'Half-stone' potatoes

1 very busy mother

1 bar of carbolic soap

1 packet of oxtail soup

Rashers/sausages

A gallon or two of water

Corned Beef and Da

Louise Phillips

It is the end of September. A vibrant sun, in hiding behind torrents of rain that has plagued the worst summer in a hundred years, has finally shown itself. I look out my bedroom window at the lush green of the Glenasmole Valley and the forests of Montpelier majestic in the distance and my body instinctively sucks and soaks, redeeming itself. The whiff of Sunday dinner drifts up the stairs amid the clamour and clatter of a family at ease with itself and somehow I am back forty years.

"Your Da's here", my mother says.

But we know that, the brute of a man, his anger seeping through the cracks in the door long before he turns the key, except of course on nights when the black stuff has been plentiful and he sits me on his knee and we laugh together like it's the most normal thing in the world. But today is Sunday and Sunday is different. Sunday Ma cooks corned beef and cabbage and Da has no work, time to think, think too much and drink but not enough.

The cups on the dresser rattle as the door closes, coffin like. The air becomes sparing, threatening. The flats are filled with families just like us, filled with mothers that cook corned beef and cabbage and fathers that finally come home. My sister, brother and I sit as unwanted additions hoping we might somehow drift into the faded flowery wallpaper of the small front room.

His eyes speak first, firing. No dinner yet, no plate filled, no place set. He is not pleased, he never is. I watch him untie his boots, big strong hands with nails of ingrained dirt and lines that mirror a rugged, ragged face. The steaming pot bellows smoke signals from the scullery, they smell of York cabbage and boiled meat and he waits. We wait. We don't eat; him first, always first. Through the corner of my eye, I watch him cut the meat, the knife upright as the food gets shoved into his almost toothless gob. Then the blind raging hateful anger that has hovered since the moment he turned the key, releases itself and spitting out the meat he roars.

"Bloody salt woman, can you do nothin' right?" And the plate with corned beef and cabbage goes flying through the air.

She says nothing, best not, not when he's like this, not ever and the door slams once more and he is gone, leaving us as castoffs in his broken wake. We sit in silence, in case, in case he might come back, bruised that way, that way children know. Later I wondered why on Sundays she always cooked the godforsaken thing and later still I learned it was his way, at least we had meat on Sundays.

Today older, through my window, I soak in the beauty of a valley hidden to me all those years before. I see the man different now. I carry his pain as he drowns his sorrow with Arthur Guinness, as he walks the tenement streets, as he faces his family, the anger of his failures weighing heavy on his shoulders. I am with him as he fires the plate, corned beef and lame cabbage and I see a life as shattered as the willow pattern on the broken plate. Then I turn and see me, a girl of eight, sad and scared. I reach down and gently take her by the hand and bring her to a place where the anger is no more.

Corned Beef and Cabbage

Ingredients:

4 lbs corned beef

6 potatoes

3 large carrots cut into chunks

2 medium onions

I cabbage

seasoning to taste.

Method:

Put the corned beef into a large pot with carrots and onions. Cover with cold water; bring to a boil. Lower the heat and simmer for an hour. From time to time, skim the fat from the top as it rises. Add the cabbage and potatoes (optional) to the pot. Cook for another one to two hours or until the meat is tender.

Plump and Succulent

Maria Blair

Auntie Nora was my mother's sister. Sisters they were but totally different in looks and personality. My mother was dark haired and Nora had flaming red hair and a temper to match. Nora never married and when her mother and father died and her brother Donal got the farm, along with a new wife, Nora came to live with us. That was the way of it.

I was an only child and we lived in the city until I was around six when we moved to the suburbs. Nora joined us in or around the same time and three became four. My mother returned to teaching – her first love and Nora basically did the housekeeping and minded me after school. What a fund of stories she had about her life growing up in West Cork. It was a totally different life – water was got from the pump about fifty yards down the road, eggs had to be collected from the hens, butter to be churned. The village post office was a focal point, being a shop also, and all the gossip of the day was regaled. From the family home, the village was West and the creamery was East. People referred to going East the road and West the road. It was a simple, uncomplicated existence. She missed it sometimes, I think, but she was a happy outgoing person and kept her thoughts to herself.

We loved one another from the start. I had not seen too much of her up to then as at that time we didn't have a car and the train journey only took us to Cork city. We then had to wait for the creamery co-op lorry to take us to Drinagh – another bone-shattering 45 miles. The roads weren't so good in those days, so our visits were a bit sporadic. However, I do remember the joys of going barefoot during the week, only putting on shoes and socks going to Mass on Sundays.

Nora and I fought a lot and laughed a lot. We were both terrible gigglers at the most inappropriate times – sometimes during the family rosary (though Nora loved her religion), when my father was expounding on some serious topic of the day, or when my mother was hearing me my multiplication tables.

Nora was a wonderful cook. Our kitchen was very small so I used to squeeze onto a stool, watch and learn. One of my all-time favourites was her rice pudding –with sultanas mixed in. They grew plump and succulent in the cooking. The mixture was topped with beaten egg and a few pinches of nutmeg and baked in the oven. To smell it cooking was divine, to eat it was mouth-wateringly delicious!

Nora died comparatively early – in her mid-seventies. She was a daily Mass goer and loved her faith in a quiet way. Practically on her death bed she told me she had been praying very hard for a special intention and had a strong feeling that God was listening. She smiled as she said this. It was one of her last smiles – she died as she had lived, uncomplainingly and left a gaping void in my life.

However, three months after she died – after eight years of marriage – my pregnancy was confirmed on my ninth wedding anniversary. It was one of the happiest moments of my life. Maybe Nora had to get to heaven first for it to happen!

Baked Rice Pudding

Preparation time: 5 minutes

Cooking Time: Fan Oven – 13/4 hours at 250?C

Serves: 2/3 people

Ingredients:

21/2 tbsp rice

¾ tbsp sugar

3 oz sultanas

Pinch of salt

¾ pint milk

1 egg (whisked)

½ tsp nutmeg

Method:

Place rice, sugar, milk, sultanas and pinch of salt in a fairly deep baking disk, stirring ingredients together. Put into a hot oven – stirring the pudding 2 or 3 times at the beginning of cooking, stirring in the skin. After approximately an hour – take out of the oven and spread whisked egg over the top – covering the whole surface. Sprinkle nutmeg on top and return to the oven for a further half to three quarters of an hour, until a skin is formed and the pudding is golden brown. Enjoy!

Lucy Daze, Lazy Days

Tony Higgins

Every pot and pan in the house has a part to play in the preparation of the banquet, even if only lined up, silver and black and yellow, like mute infantry men, in serried lines upon the living room carpet.

The cook's helper (me) has to squat on the floor to work at the right level, and it is not easy, reminding me of just how exhausting it can be helping to raise a delightful child, whose only flaws are night- time leg cramps probably caused by too active days, and a vivid imagination that seemingly knows no limitations, and frequently takes us on *drives* to Africa or Australia to visit her various menageries.

I duly sample the 'chicken salad' soup, stir endlessly the batches of fairy cakes, adding flavours as instructed, and taste the endless streams of pasta. There are lots and lots of pasta, possibly hinting at an Italian gene hidden remotely in the cook's lineage. It does not matter a bit that the soup is water, the main ingredient of the fairy cakes is plastic alphabet letters and the pasta ranges in shape and colour from stubby pencils and crayons, to old burst balloons, each moment is treated with a fierce intensity as the preparation progresses.

And the climax is the birthday cake, complete with imaginary icing and invisible candles, which is finally ready, just in time to be presented with fanfare and eyes shining with love as Mother comes through the front door.

In contrast, I recall hearing a recent terse exchange as child and mother struggled through an over familiar book just before bed time. For the sake of education and variety Mother tried to introduce a few words in the Irish language.

"Madra", she said, pointing at the animal on the appropriately dog-eared page. "Madra", she repeated, pointing again.

The child raised a weary and slightly wary eye.

"He's a dog," she said. " Just call him dog." And we both struggled to stifle our laughter which might be misinterpreted by a tired and sensitive child. It reminded me of another recent dialogue in August also. A nice lady trying to making polite conversation with Lucy asked "And when will you be four? Briefly, my mind jumbled with a number beyond twenty and the names of months barely ever mentioned. How would Lucy cope with an answer well beyond her experience? Once again, I realised how quickly time flies. "When I am finished being three," Lucy replied with the same admirable precision she brings to her bouts of 'baking'.

The slow, nothing happening days trickle by, becoming a cascade of splendid, small moments which pool as years around our feet, each isolated incident in danger of floundering and drowning in the swift tide called everyday life.

In the words of the old, less than famous, song:-

" The mile-stones of a life time are hidden on the ground,

They only look like high- lights when you pause to look around".

And the scent shifts west to Mayo where we are 'holidaying', held indoors by the weather. It continues to rain outside. The cousins tumble through the house in raucous games of hide and seek. Outside, six sparrows line themselves in a mute chorus line along the garden fence, as they watch for household scraps. I doubt if they are complaining about the weather.

Womb Pampering with Yam and Pepper Soup

Vanessa Ogida

Weeeeeeeeeee, weeeeeeeee,weeee, the cry of a bundle of joy - the arrival of an additional member to the Osagie family.

Amoogun! Amoogun! the ladies from the Sisters' Circle Club cried to their fellow member, who had just been delivered of a bouncing baby boy.

The atmosphere charged up as more and more visitors came in. The kitchen was steaming with all sorts of dishes including yam and pepper soup for the newest mummy.

Mmm, the thought of yam and pepper soupbrought those memories rushing into my head. Indeed, the memories of childbirth and the pampering afterwards.

Yam and pepper soup is a delicious African delicacy specially used in pampering women who have just put to birth. Sometimes, I wonder why it has to be served with pepper soup. Just in case you do not know what pepper soup is, it is a kind of soup with a lot of chili in it. Chili again? After labour pains, chilli? But you know what? We couldn't do without it, after a childbirth!

Yam and Pepper Soup Meal from Nigeria

Ingredients:

1 tuber of yam

pepper soup spice

Knorr/Maggi cube

salt to taste

fish/ chicken/beef/offal (gwogwo/kayan cikin)

Method:

Cut and wash whatever your choice of meat or fish is. Leave to drain in a colander.

Peel and cut yam into desired size. Place a pot with 1 litre of water on the burner,

bring to the boil (if using other choices of meat except fish,place in the pot as you bring to boil, this is because meat takes longer to cook). If using fish, place yam in a pot of boiling water to cook for 15 minutes. Add pepper soup spice, Knorr cube, dry pepper and salt to taste. Taste to see if the seasoning is okay. Add fish, leave to cook for another 10-15 minutes.

First Taste

Karah Berber

Irish Smoked Salmon was always a speciality at my gran's house for parties and family celebrations. Gran would serve it many different ways, thin slices with the lovely bright colours of salad leaves, tomatoes and peppers – delicious.

Even in a simple sandwich the taste, colour and rich smell brings back happy memories of the first time I tasted smoked salmon at my gran's house.

Serve thin slices of Irish Smoked Salmon with any combination of salad leaves and don't forget juicy tomatoes and peppers for colour.

Irish Smoked Salmon at my Gran's

Ingredients:

One very creative Grandmother

A party or family celebration

Lots of lovely bright colours

Juicy tomatoes

Peppers

Salad leaves

The rich smell of happiness.

Loaves and Fishes

Frank Price

Born into a family of eleven brothers and four sisters, I was the youngest of the family. We lived in a Corporation house in Kimmage, Dublin 12. This was a two bedroom home with parlour and kitchen downstairs. My early memories are of my mother cooking on the oven over the fireplace. On a Saturday, it was always steak and kidney pie for dinner. This pie seemed to last forever, as it fed all of us. When I got older I got the recipe from my mother who taught me how to make it. I now make it for my children and grandchildren. I have eight children, four girls and twenty-three grandchildren. Yet the pie continues to last forever as they come to me on Saturdays and all get a share.

Steak and Kidney Pie

Ingredients:

1lb round steak

1 tsp mixed herbs

Oxo cubes

1 heaped tbsp Bisto

1 pint water

oil

½ cup of flour

Pastry mix:

12 ozs self-raising flour

6 oz butter

¼ pint milk and water

Method:

Place ½ cup flour and mixed herbs seasoning in a bowl. Dice the steak and kidney (1inch cubes) and mix in the flour. Place the pan on a moderate heat and add the oil. Fry the steak dices until brown, about five minutes. Add the 2 Oxo cubes to the pan. Add the flour from the bowl to the pan and let it soak up all the oil. Make sure the flour is well blended. Add the Bisto to 1 pint water and mix well. Then add to the pan making a rich gravy. Place the mix into a Pyrex or oven square dish.

Pastry mix:

Place the flour into a bowl and knead in the butter until it is well blended. Add the water and milk together, slowly, until there is firm dough. Flour the table or board and roll out the dough to a ½ inch thick. Place over the mix in the Pyrex dish and place in the oven, gas mark 5 for forty-five minutes, until the pastry is nice and brown. Serve with potatoes, carrots and peas.

Russian Pel'meni (pill-Main-yi)

Lyuba Koroleva Moore

This is the festive speciality of the Ural Mountains and Siberia. So much folklore is associated with these ravioli-like titbits that it is hard to know where to begin. For starters, the word itself is from the Udmurt language, the native speech of the original inhabitants of the part of Russia where I grew up, Udmurtia. In Udmurt the word means "ear bread", which is something that's easy to understand when you see the finished product, which starts out as a crimped half-moon with its meat filling, but is then twisted into a little flying-saucer shaped object. If this is beginning to sound labour-intensive, it is. This is where the second folkloric element comes in.

Making *pel'meni* is normally a family affair, roping in as many people as you can to make huge quantities, some of which are then cooked,, but most of which are preserved in the freezer – which normally used to mean just outside the winter kitchen window, in a burlap bag. We're talking about deepest Russia, here! We all have freezers, now, and can enjoy these wonderful things both winter and summer. I'll give the ingredients for a smaller amount than usual, on the grounds that cooking tends to be so much a solitary affair in this country, these days. But bear in mind that sons or daughters home from school can be usefully employed, usually to their delight, in the actual stuffing and twisting that results in the finished product.

Ingredients:

For a meal for four people, with some left over to fry up for a Russian-style breakfast the next day, include:

For the pasta-dough shells:

1 kg (2.24 lbs, about 36 oz. or half a normal package) of regular strong white flour, 1 egg,

1 glass of (very) cold water, salt (a pinch or less – the classic pel'meni has no salt in the dough at all).

For the meat stuffing:

300 g (10-11 oz.) of beef, 300 g (10-11 oz.) of pork or 300 g (10-11 oz.) of lamb, if pork is undesirable, 1 large or 2 small onions, salt and pepper as desired

The meat must be finely ground up, together with the onions, salt, and pepper. Old-style meat-grinders are rarely seen here in Ireland, but using ready-ground beef won't produce the desired texture, and ground pork or lamb is nearly impossible to find. So – if you have a food-processor, then use it so that the final product is extremely finely chopped and blended into one undifferentiated mass. Or if you're lucky enough to have an old-style meat grinder, pass the whole lot through the grinder at least twice to achieve the desired consistency.

To make the dough for the pasta, first sieve the whole lot of the flour onto your work-top, in a single mound; then make a crater in the center of the hillock for your egg. With a fork, gently mix the lot, starting in the center, adding a few splashes or drops of your cold water every few minutes (NOT all at once!); once it appears to be fairly mixed, then dig in with your (floured) hands, kneading the mass at least 5-10 min. until it appears to be elastic and stops sticking to your fingers. Like any dough, it should then be left to rest for about half an hour, wrapped up in a damp cloth – gaining a bit of elasticity.

Then divide the dough into four pieces and roll them out one by one as you use them up: roll each piece as thin as you can, normally about 2mm, and cut out circles with a cookie-cutter or a glass or cup with an 8-cm (3 in.) mouth. Get as many of the circles as you can from each piece, since the re-rolling of the dough to use up the scrap pieces ordinarily results in the dough taking on more flour and losing elasticity.

Now comes the part involving the helpers: picking up a circle of dough in your left hand, place a teaspoonful of the stuffing into the centre of your circle; close your fist on it and carefully pinch the edges together, so that you have a half-moon of stuffed centre and flattened edge. Then pull the two ends together and pinch to make little Saturn-shaped objects, as in the picture, a ball of stuffing with a tilted platter of pinched dough around it. These you place one-by-one on a floured platter until you have exhausted all your ingredients. Dump them, a couple dozen at a time, into a pot of water that has already been brought to boil. The pot of salty water on the boil with a couple of bay leaves floating in it. When each lot of *pel'meni* have all floated to the surface, they are done. They should be removed from the boiling water with a slotted spoon, and the next lot put in.

Traditionally, the cook serves the assembled eaters each portion of cooked *pel'meni* as they are removed from the pot, but in modern times a large, heated serving dish can be filled up with the successive portions and the lot eaten at one go. Also traditionally the dumplings are eaten by spearing them with a fork and dipping them into a bowl of vinegar. This is a little extreme in the gastronomic West, where pretty much any condiment (including the wonderful balsamic vinegar, soya sauce, or hot Thai-style chilli sauce) can be used as the final element in the progression.

Long Hallways in Wroclaw

Anna Sudol

When I was maybe ten years old, I remember a freezing winter's day. My mum let me go out to play to a nearby hill with my best friend and her younger brother. My dad gave me the sled and Mum dressed me up warm to go out. With my friend Julia and her brother we were told we should go to a really close by little hill (man-made), which was beside our apartments in a street called Sliczna (which means 'beautiful' in translation). Instead we went to a forbidden high hill, far away from home. So we had to walk a long while and when we got to it, we enjoyed ourselves one hundred per cent. There was lots of snow around us and sleds on which we slid down the hill for hours. But after a long while had gone by, our parents started looking for us and we started to freeze. When our parents found us, we were in big trouble. However, Mum saw how cold we were and set about preparing our favourite, pierogi.

Another bad history happened around that time also, when I was ten. All the children were playing outside and the older children got the idea of playing hide n' seek inside our building under the ground floor. It was really dark there. I remember that on all the buildings there were twelve long halls with about two or three lamps. There were lots of hiding places. When I was searching for my friends I banged my head on a really hard wall and I needed go to the doctor. Of course I got into trouble at home, yet again. Because I was in pain poor mum, although angry with me for being foolish and playing in a dangerous way, made me comforting pierogi.

When I was about fifteen, a close friend, Marlena, committed suicide. She was one year older then me and she had her first boyfriend then. He broke up with her and she made the biggest mistake of her life, her last…. She took her mum's pills for a heart complaint and she never woke up. Even after these years, everybody from her group of family and friends remember her and I think now this is all what we can do for her. I'm afraid all the pierogi in Poland would not comfort a loss like that.

I suppose food and good memories then are what makes the connection for me. Like the times when my dad was teaching me how to ride a bike. That was fabulous, despite all the falling down. My first bike was red and I had it a short time, because I had so many accidents. One of those was to finish up on a tree trunk, when I was speeding. All those cut knees and scrapes were soothed away by Mum's pierogi treats. In the summer, my dad always took me on bike trips to the river Olawaka which was far away from home. Because we cycled so far, more than two hours, I was always coming back with little burns or 'sun kisses' from the sun. Christmas dinner is another example of happy times. It was great fun preparing all the food because on a Polish Christmas table there might be twelve kinds of food with no meat in it, only fish. And of course my favourite beetroot soup with fresh mushrooms and cabbage. Gorgeous!

Pierogi

Ingredients:

For pasta: flour, one or two eggs, boiled but cold flour water.

For stuffing: mashed potatoes, cottage cheese, fry onion, little of mashed garlic, oil, black pepper and little salt.

Method:

First, prepare pasta cake. Make sure there is a roller to hand before making. Three-quarters of a bag of flour put on the table, make the little hole in the middle, next put on one or two eggs inside and a little water. You must make not dry, but not too liquid cake, so add water but avoid a sticky consistency. Next use the roller to make the cake flat, around 3mm in thickness. A big table is needed for this. Take a cup and cut out round circles on this cake. There should now just be pasta circles. Put some flour under the cake, so it won't stick.

Turn for stuffing. Mashed potatoes mix with onion fried in oil. Add cottage cheese and take a spoon and mix it. Add mashed garlic and pepper with a little bit of salt. Mix all and leave in the fridge for half hour.

Now take pasta circles in your hand and put on the middle a spoon of stuffing. Try to close by closing your hand, and stick cake around the edges with your fingers. Make sure there is no gap around the edges, otherwise the stuffing will come out when cooking. Into boiling water throw a few of them at a time and make sure that they don't stick to the bottom of the pan. When they start rising, they are ready. Enjoy!

My Rite of Passage

Tanzeela Azeem

About seven years back, when I was thirteen, I entered the kitchen to cook food for the first time. It was a nice sunny day in Pakistan and everybody was on holiday. It was Sunday and I told my dad and mom that I wanted to cook food that day. Then I entered the kitchen. I was all alone and nervous, a little, but I had seen my mom cook lots of times. I started to peel the vegetables. I imagined that my mom and dad were noticing me and I was again nervous thinking that all my family members were noticing me. I was scared and full of doubts that I wouldn't cook well. Then, I took a deep breath and did the same as I had noticed my mom doing, from the beginning. I did the same, keeping everything in my mind. I got many small cuts on my hand and I burnt my arm on one side but I succeeded in cooking and then cleaning the kitchen. Oh my God! Was that a big job! But it was enjoyable.

When I went out of the kitchen I was surprised. My aunts and uncles and cousins were out there. I was shocked too. They gave me a surprise for sure and we were all very happy. I was also feeling happy because I saw how important I was that day, it was a lucky day. My biryani was delicious all of them said and from then until now I was always given the responsibility of cooking this dish on every good day of our lives. In short, it was a very good experience. I was noticed and given a surprise from my family, who I really miss these days. Here ends my story. Be happy, make others laugh. This is life. Enjoy it a lot, count your blessings.

Chicken Biryani

It depends on how many people you are going to cook for. But always remember that if you are making the dish for a large amount of people you will need more quantity of things and for less amount of people, you will need about half of the things.

This recipe will serve ten to twenty.

Ingredients:

8 – 10 onions (normal size)

12 tomatoes (normal size)

5 green chillies

2 large chickens (cut in pieces)

2 packs of biryani masala

8 cups of rice

oil as needed

To prepare:

Add oil to a pan and bring it up to a warm temperature, then chop onions and add them in. Fry until golden brown and then chop and add tomatoes and green chillies. Add the packs of biryani masala and cook very well until onions and tomatoes are mixed and mashed well. On another pan, fry the chicken until a little golden brown. Fry potato chips and add them for more nice taste. Boil rice but don't allow it to be fully boiled, for a maximum 10 – 12 minutes. Then add the fried chicken to the mixture of onions and tomatoes, cook for about 15 minutes.

Remove the rice and dry off the water in a basin, then take a big container and add a part of the rice first with a spoon, making a layer then adding the chicken and again the rice – alternatively. Add the last rice on top and fry a small onion little brown to also add on top. Keep it on a very slow flame for 20 to 25 minutes and then your chicken biryani is ready! Serve hot. To add more flavour serve with yogurt. Enjoy the meal with your friends and pray for us.

The Ulster Fry

Mae Newman

Fasting from midnight on Saturday night to receive Holy Communion at Mass on Sunday, meant breakfast was a big event in our house. There was no dawdling on The Diamond steps or hanging around Peter's Box, hoping to find a penny to buy sweets. My mother went to first Mass, children to second and my father went to last.Saturday night was exceptionally busy as we had to have a bath, clean underwear ready for morning, polish shoes, steep peas and make jellies. The shops stayed open until ten so all our country relatives came to do their weekly shopping, stopping at our house for tea.

Sunday was a relaxing day for everyone except mammy. Potato bread was my all time favourite. Mammy made this but if times were good, Daddy bought some. These were made by Galbraith's of Dundalk and were truly delicious. The other must have, was soda farl. This was basically the same as soda breadbut made on a griddle pan on top of the black range. In the summer time my brother was sent out to Jaunty Myer's field to gather mushrooms before Mass. You had to be early as half the town would be out with their buckets. With rasher, sausages and black and white pudding, sometimes we had to make do with duck eggs. Most eggs were smuggled across the border into the North.

There were certain advantages to living in a border town. All roads, except one out of Clones led to the North. Smuggling was a way of life for us. We never looked on it as doing wrong. The approved roads had custom huts on them. The unapproved roads were much better once you knew which side you were on. Except these roads were patrolled by the B Specials, who were a totally different breed from the Custom men.

With their shiny black boots and their gun they'd put the fear of God into you. They'd never believe you weren't carrying cigarettes and insist on questioning you. Sometimes the Northern and Free State custom huts were in spitting distance of one another. After World War Two there was a severe shortage of most goods. Food was rationed and you had to produce a ration book with each purchase. Bread was the one thing we shopped for in the North every day. We'd take a child for a walk so that we could fill the pram with delicious white bread, not like the grey stuff we had in the South. Butter was tricky, if travelling by train, as it had to be hidden on the body and as happened to my mother, could melt down the front of your dress.

Potato Bread

Ingredients:

1 cup flour

1 cup cold mashed potato

½ cup melted butter

pinch of salt and pepper

Method:

Mix together to form a soft dough. Roll out thinly with rolling pin. Cut into triangles and fry until golden brown.

Chicken Beryani.....is for Happiness

Anas Al Saadi

I am thirty-six years old and an Iraqi national. My family consists of five persons, my father, mother, brother and my twin sister. Now I am married, with two daughters, Yamama aged eight and Hajar aged one. I am an experienced Arabic and Chinese Chef. My experience in hotel business exceeds seven years. I also have a Bachelor's Degree in Hotel Management – major Food and Beverage. Perhaps my career path is due to the rules surrounding food that my father set to us, rules like:

We have to help my mom prepare the table.

We have to respect breakfast, lunch and dinner time, all five of us have to be there to start eating, this means if I came early from my school I have to wait until everybody else is there.

We have to take three main courses; breakfast, lunch and dinner.

We have to finish the whole food in our dish and not throw any away.

We have to help in cleaning the table and washing the dishes.

We are not allowed to refuse any kind of food provided; all food is healthy and good for our body.

Beryani with chicken is our favourite, it is also an Iraqi famous dish, it is not difficult to make. Beryani is often served on different occasions, happy ones not sad ones. Each occasion has its own dish; beryani is served for birthday parties, engagement parties, weddings and completion of school or university. We invite relatives and friends on different occasions and we serve beryani as the main dish. The last time I cooked beryani was on 26th April 2008 this date was my daughter's first birthday, which was the second happy event for me in Ireland, the first one was her birthday (Thursday, 26th April 2007).

Chicken Beryani

Ingredients:

basmati rice

noodles (special eastern thin ones)

chicken

cooking ghee or sunflower cooking oil

sesame oil (for flavour)

potato, onion, carrots, beans, raisins, boiled egg spices (salt, red pepper, black pepper, cinnamon, cloves, cardamom, coriander, mint leaves, ginger and saffron)

Preparation:

Wash the chicken, remove the bones and chop it to pieces. Put it into a pot and add water, add some salt, cinnamon, cloves, cardamom and coriander. Cook until done. Remove the chicken from the pot, drain and keep aside.

Wash the rice in a sieve. Heat some ghee or cooking oil in a cooking pot, add the rice and enough chicken water to fully cover the rice Add salt to taste. Add all the spices mentioned above. Set the rice up to boil. Once boiled, leave it on a light stove fire. Add some sesame oil for the flavour. Cook till almost done. To determine when it has reached that stage, remove a few grains from the pot and press between your thumb and forefinger. The rice should mostly mash but will have a firm whitish core. Turn off the fire.

Garnish:

Peel the potato cut it into small cubes then fry it in a frying pan until cooked, then drain and keep aside in a large mixing pot.

Method:

Cut the onion into thin slices, heat a little oil in a pan and fry the onion until it becomes golden brown, drain and keep in the large mixing pot with the potato.

Heat a little oil in a pan and fry the raisins for a few seconds, drain and keep in the large mixing pot. Peel the carrots, chop into small cube pieces, boil it with water and salt along with the beans, until well cooked. Drain and put it with the other ingredients on the mixing pot. Heat a little oil in a pan and fry the noodles until they become golden brown, add some chicken water and leave for 5 minutes until well cooked. Drain and add to the other ingredients in the mixing pot. Mix all the ingredients in the mixing pot, add all the spices mentioned above in small quantities (tasting all the time). Heat a little oil and fry the well boiled eggs until they become golden. Cut into slices and keep aside.

Now all the ingredients are ready to be served, put the rice first on a large serving plate, then add the mixed ingredients above the rice, and then garnish with the sliced egg.

Flavours of Home

Premise and Process

To celebrate 2008, the Year of Intercultural Dialogue, a series of workshops in key areas; Tallaght, Lucan and Clondalkin, took place during the months June/July. The initiative was structured and supported by The Social Inclusion Unit, South Dublin County Council. Therefore, the chief aims were to break down barriers between race, culture and gender and to provide a space where integration could flourish. The smooth flow of each individual workshop owed much to the organisational skills of Maria Finn, Senior Staff Officer with the Social Inclusion Unit. When I first broached Maria about the premise of the publication, she whole-heartedly embraced the idea, broadening and extending it to include children as well as adults. The artwork for the cover of the publication was obtained through open competition in local schools.

The objective of the workshops was to bring together participants in a relaxed, informal space. By so doing, it was possible to create an atmosphere of trust and respect. Most of all, the structure of the workshops was geared towards enjoyment. Personal memory, connected with the sharing of food, would prove memorable and insightful for all. Throughout this sharing process, there was a tremendous sense of empathy for each participant's unique story. Each story was generously shared. It soon became clear that although there are indeed different cultures, with their own rituals and traditions, the 'global' family at its very core, has much in common.

Accessing Family History (Opening the storehouse of memory)

In order to access family history in the workshops I decided to use the visual aid of a storyboard. First of all, it would enable me to share some of my own family history and show the importance food has in many universal areas, ranging through literature, film, art. I began with the personal however, and showed a photograph of my mother having a good 'belly laugh' (I cannot remember the reason!) at my nephew's Christening party nearly thirty four years ago. I love the photograph, it shows the happy days. I have a photograph of myself at thirteen with my mother and my dog Prince, an adorable sheepdog.

In 2005 I visited St. Brigid's well, Liscannor, Co. Clare and took a photograph of a nest of swallows perched atop a Holy picture in the grotto. I used the example of the 'swallow family' to illustrate how, though family members leave, they come back again. Before the workshops commenced I had a visit from my brother Noel and his family who now live in South Carolina, USA. I photographed us all together again on a sunny day in June in Old

Bawn, Tallaght around the table. I had prepared a feast and made tea with tea leaves all the way from Iran that my lovely friend Lynda Tavakoli gave me. Lo and behold, atop one of the cups floated a smiling face made of tea-leaves. I photographed it (naturally) and used that to highlight this more contemporary happy memory. I spoke about my humble beginnings in a two-up, two-down council house and showed a grainy black and white photograph of my mother as a young woman standing outside the back door with her brood. Although it shows that I did not come from a wealthy background in monetary terms (indeed, far from it), I'm proud of my roots. On the storyboard I pinned also a receipt from a local supermarket showing the cost of groceries (we can all relate to these regular receipts!) but more importantly being able to identify certain characters from my family from the items bought. Food preferences abound, was there ever a truer statement; "One man's meat is another's poison"? Whatever decisions we make, family wellbeing is never far behind.

I included a postcard by Renoir 'Breakfast of the Rowers', a particular favourite of mine. I just love its colour and vivacity. I mentioned that evocative poem 'Quoof' by Paul Muldoon which demonstrates how each family have their own intimate relationship with language. In my own family history, we got bread mashed up with hot milk in a cup before going to bed and called the dish 'goodie'. In his contribution 'My Mother's Soup Kitchen', Mervyn Ennis makes reference to a 'yark' of butter, a word unique to that family. I had recently watched *Babette's Feast* (Isak Dinesen) and through that, was able to relay the nurturing elements of food and how eating well in convivial company can erase the 'greyness' which envelopes us at times. Food is both evocative and sensual. No mention of literature in relation to food would be complete without Joanne Harris's *Chocolat* or James Joyce's 'The Dead' from *Dubliners*. I read from Brian Keenan's *An Evil Cradling*, the part where he sees oranges, having been in the darkness of captivity for such a long time. Keenan conveys the nurturing and holistic effect of colour, an element sometimes taken for granted 'such absolute wonder in such an insignificant fruit':

The colour orange, my God the colour orange. Before me is a feast of colour. I feel myself begin to dance, slowly. I am intoxicated by colour. I feel the colour in a quiet somnambulist rage. Such wonder, such absolute wonder in such an insignificant fruit.

Having 'broken the ice', the participants were invited to open the storehouse of memory and given certain triggers such as 'the best meal', 'the worst meal', 'three things about family life', ' a ritual or a celebration' connected with family meals and so on. Writing through the senses proved especially effective. Food has many flavours but there's lots of texture, smell, visual, that all important taste and of course all that bubbling, hissing, splattering, boiling up, percolating etc. make for fantastic sound effects! The key to opening memory can appear in many guises. In this way, 'snapshots' were taken of family life, all of them vivid and memorable.

Family life is an important element in any society. Different cultural communities coming together and engaging in dialogues surrounding family life is indeed a bonding process. Every family, no matter where in the world, knows the ordinary of the day to day, the trials, tribulations and the celebratory occasions also. All of the workshops were inspirational and thought provoking. Each location yielded its own treasury of family history and there was a great sense of opening that treasury, for the first time in many cases. Tallaght's workshop took place in the refurbished County Library. Stories ranged from the making of cassava in the Congo, a first experience of eating steak and onions at the age of seven right through to the politics of food. The struggle of a Nigerian Woman, Omolola Alorge to persuade her son Festos to eat healthily, 'A Tale of Two Sons, is a universal one. Irishman Brian Kirk in his contribution 'A Small Tyranny' revisits this scenario from the perspective of an adult who was once a 'difficult' eater, forging a universal connection. Anne Cleary tells in 'Courgette Soup' a tale of stealth and perseverance in getting vegetables into her young twin daughters Bo and Lotti. Maria Petrovicheva McManus, originally from Vnukoa, Russia, tells of the 'struggle' her dad and her cat endured when housekeepers were scarce and cucumbers abundant in her piece ' The Cucumber Season'.

The Clondalkin workshop took place in The Civic Offices situated near The Towers, currently a refuge for Asylum Seekers. Because of the workshop, participants who live in The Towers were allowed to cook food in the kitchen in the Towers for the first time since coming to Ireland. This proved an emotional exercise but a very fulfilling one. The food that these men and women brought to the table in Clondalkin was without parallel. Martha, from Mexico, told us how her young son Josef found it so hard to settle here until she painstakingly learnt how to make the Mexican dish (Tortillas) he so loved. Her labour of love involved many phone calls home and many attempts (there is a particular knack in making the pastry) before getting it right. A mother's love knows no bounds. Tanzeela from Pakistan brought a colourful rice dish and told of her rite of passage from child to young woman through learning how it was made. She now had responsibilities. Other participants who contributed so generously to the success of the Clondalkin workshop came from as far away as Iraq and The Democratic Republic of Congo. Graham Carry (Manager of The Towers) brought his grandmother's memory to life through his telling of a story centred around her brown bread recipe. Again, as in Tallaght, there was a great atmosphere of trust, enjoyment and above all, empathy and respect.

In all three workshops, there was a strong representation from Ireland. Earlier in the year, 'Doors are for Opening' was held to celebrate International Day against Racism, 2008. It was good to welcome into the workshops participants who had featured in this initiative with the submission of powerful writing.

The Lucan Workshop was held in Lucan Library, a very welcoming venue. Countries featuring on the afternoon in question included Nigeria, Somalia and Ireland. The stories that unfolded once more created an environment where the storehouse of memory translated itself into a universal narrative. This was another success in terms of intercultural dialogue. Family portraits emerged, brought to vivid illustration through each participant's willingness to share family history and experience. Vanessa from Nigeria spoke about a ceremony which renewed family loyalties at the start of the New Year. The positive benefits of this ceremony rippled out into the larger community. Joan Power added a great big burst of humour telling of her newly married bliss and the making of home brew! Ladies from Mogadishu, Somalia, provided a roll-call of honour for their nation, Leila Mudei, Fadumo Ibrahim, Coashu Digabe, Sarah Fabrah, Leyla Abdi. Sarah told of how, since coming to Ireland, she keeps herself very focused and motivated. She hopes to study to become a nurse, that is her goal. She has a great interest in local history also. Sarah helped her kinswoman Coashu tell her story, of sharing her food with her neighbour in Lucan and through that act, feeling a sense of belonging. Coashu made the very telling observation that drumming in Mogadishu and the dancing that accompanies it, is very similar to Irish dancing! She knew about Michael Flatley also! Coashu brought along a delicious dish for us to sample, beautifully cooked and presented, consisting of rice and meat.

Through Faduma we learnt that the cooking of semolina (Sor) has a class connotation in Somalia. Semolina is cooked for the family and would never be offered to invited guests, purely because it is not meat-based. Those who eat meat are perceived as being 'better-off' and would belong to farming communities. Leila told of her experiences of learning to cook Halwa, a sweet dish used for parties or weddings. Her mother taught her this dish in response to Leila's request to learn how to cook. Following the Lucan workshop, an item reporting the event appeared in the Lucan Newsletter, from Michael Finnegan;

"In particular Michael congratulates South Dublin County Council for organising a very successful workshop held in the Lucan Library on Tuesday 22nd July. This was organised by the Social Inclusion Unit Senior Staff Officer Maria Finn, and was very skilfully handled by Eileen Casey who involved all the workshop participants" –Lucan Newsletter

The workshops were a real pleasure. Friendships were made, insights exchanged but above all, the importance of family life from a local and global perspective was highlighted through the power of story. At its very core, society, no matter how diverse culturally, has a shared narrative. As a result, doors were opened in hearts, minds and spirits.

Eileen Casey

Through the Glass Brightly

Marie Gahan

Growing up in the 'Hungry Fifties' mass unemployment dogged our childhood. At school, the teacher's question, "Is your father working" was more relevant than the nature of his job. My big sister, Kathleen joined the hordes of young people, taking the B & I boat to England each week. She found work in a cotton mill in Bolton in Lancashire.

In our house, hand-me-down clothes and plain food were the order of the day. Bread and jam was a firm favourite, managing to fill us and satisfy a sweet tooth as well. Mam was a very basic cook, but in hindsight, I realise that it was lack of finance that stinted her style. Filling bellies took precedence over titillating palettes. Oh how we loved when she made a tray of fruit slices. Gur Cake we called it. It was cheap, filling and nourishing as well. Homeless people 'out on gur' could buy it by the slice for a ha'penny in any of the little bakeries or shops in Dublin.

She'd steep some dried fruit, currants, raisins or sultanas in milk and add sugar and broken up bread. Then, she'd drop in a chopped cooking apple and add mixed spice, sometimes nutmeg, if she had it. Finally, she'd add a dollop of molasses, give the whole thing a good mixing and let it stand while she was rolling out the pastry. We'd watch as she spooned the gooey mix onto the bottom layer and cover it with the other. I'll always remember the warm spicy smell emanating from the gas stove, flooding the kitchen and meeting us at the front door. When it was baked, she'd put it on the table to cool. We couldn't wait for her to cut it up into little squares. We'd bite into it, soft sweet fruit oozing out of the corners of the golden pastry.

Mam had got the recipe from her own mother, who started making gur cake during the Great Lockout in 1913, when the gates of the Dublin Gas Company were closed to my grandfather and his fellow workers. The ingredients were cheap. The main purchase was the dried mixed fruit. Milk and sugar would have been in the house anyway. There was a good chance of mixed spice or nutmeg being left over from the Christmas pudding. Best of all, it recycled stale bread. No wonder Dubliners took to it as their own.

The economic boom of the seventies brought all sorts of delicacies to my kitchen table, yet gur cake remained a firm favourite with my two young daughters. Nowadays, I bake it for my two little grandsons. They love putting on their aprons, running the fruit through their fingers, stirring the gooey mixture and making a mess. Then they watch their 'work of art' bake through the glass oven door.

"Is it ready yet, Nana, is it ready yet?"

Then Granddad arrives home from work and says, "Goodee, gur cakes for tea!"

Gur Cake

Ingredients for filling mix:

1 packet of dried mixed fruit

½ pint milk

3 slices of stale bread

2 tbsp of sugar

1 to 2 tsp of mixed spice or nutmeg

1 large cooking apple

A good dollop of molasses

Method:

Roll out two sheets of pastry to fit a flat oven tray. Sandwich the filling mix between them and bake in a medium oven for 30 minutes or until golden brown. Allow to cool, then cut into squares.

My Mother's Soup Kitchen

Mervyn Ennis

In those days the hedgerows and trees around Ballymount provided the tinder for the fire and Mother would coax and protect the gentle flame into a sustained heat to cook, roast or boil, without regulators, but with the intuitive wave of her hand around the oven or over the plates as my mother juggled pots depending on the approximate time for cooking their contents; potatoes, cabbage, turnips, parsnips, celery, or cake tins. Like a magician she wove daily spells to feed her demanding brood.

There was no fancy culinary vocabulary as exists today - words like a drizzle of oil, a sautee, a medley of, garnish, marinate, effuse. Her words were a 'yark' of country butter, a handful of parsley, a snatch of thyme, a sprinkle of salt, a few carrots, a couple of onions and a load of spuds. The only thing fancy was the taste. The proof of her soup or cooking was in her boast that "You'd get up in the night to eat it, or it would bring you back from the dead". Her Irish stew was derived from rib steak and lap mutton, the quantity of the steak depended on the weight of her purse and what it could afford. But there was no scarcity on the volume of vegetables as we were self sufficient and grew our own. That is the true meaning of' Sinn Fein' you grow your own and depend as little as possible on others, she'd advise. The steak was diced except for my father's portion, it had to be kept whole and hopefully it didn't shrivel in the pot as she often claimed. Kidneys or liver could be added depending on how generous the butcher was or what he had as special.

On Fridays, she might head into town on the bus, first by cycling to Walkinstown where she had a choice of buses, 50 A or B, 54, 55, 56, rather then depend on the infrequent no. 77. The hidden attraction was to meet Molly or Annie, two dealers in the Market just off Capel Street for a natter as much as a bargain. Memory does not serve me well as to the names of the various dealers but Molly and Annie leap out at me, for as a child of 9 or 10 I was sent into to tell "Molly who I was and be sure they give you a good bargain." She'd arrive home with a parcel of various types of fish, and maybe three or four chickens. Two of these chickens would be rendered down and boiled while the other would be kept for roasting on Sunday with a bit of bacon and cabbage.

On mature reflection these were not the water filled foreign fowl one gets today. These were some seasoned champions from a country farm yard. Used to trumpeting in a new day, and scratching and scraping around the farm yard or paddocks and sampling the cattle's grains and hops or the pigs nuts and swill. These fowl were Olympians compared to the water babies of today. Their tendons may have snapped like bow strings but the soup they prepared matched their free range status. It was not unusual for the hind quarter of a rabbit to be added to the boil and if offered as a drumstick one would be undistinguishable from a chicken leg. After a day's shooting, some plover might join the fowl, and when eating we were warned not to watch for bones but for lead pellets.

After getting the meat from the butcher, mother would cajole him for a few marrow bones. These were large leg bones that the butcher sawed up with a large wooden handled hack saw he hung on a huge hook for the beef, sheep and pig carcasses. When Ronnie Drew sang about the benefits of sucking 'eggs and marrow bones' we knew what he meant. The bones were boiled maybe with a knuckle of mutton and a portion of lap. It would melt down into the mixture. The bones were then removed and the mixture allowed to set. This would stand as soup in its own right, but when a variety of vegetables is added and cooked over a gentle heat they disintegrate. Added barley then pumped up the mixture. The spuds were always cooked on their own and could be added later or mashed depending on the choice of different family members, or kept for a few chops or a bit of steak and onions for the 'auld fella'. He was always 'on special'.

The process was always the same for chicken, lamb, beef stew or vegetable. Indeed Mother's vegetable soup was not vegetarian. Fish was equally cooked on the bone, boiled or fried. But when stewed, was issued with a warning 'mind the bones some of them might have gotten through the strainer'. I was into my adulthood when introduced to chowder but it wasn't a patch on my ma's creamed fish stew compliments of Molly and Annie. Has Irish cuisine arrived? No they just put fancy phrases on the wholesome goodness we were always used to.

Tacos in Ireland

Martha Sanchez O'Connell

I remember the first time I cooked this sooo. ..Mexican dish. Finding the ingredients in Dublin was kind of difficult, but eventually I found them and my family and I made a party at home. I was not very sure if our guests were going to like them, because it's kind of messy eating them, unless you separate the salad from the tacos.   But fortunately they did. I was very surprised to find out that many of our friends liked the spicy salsa… I remember telling each one of them "the salsa is very hot", but still they tried it and they were really pleased to eat it.

The most important element of that day was that even when we were so far away from our country we could feel ourselves enjoying something that is very popular in Mexico. Mexico is a very big country and no matter where you go, you can find fried tacos everywhere!

For me, just the simple smell of the lettuce, cucumber and red onion with some sea salt and lemon, takes me back home, I can close my eyes and no matter where I am, I can picture myself in my mother's kitchen, sitting on the dining- table, picking some cucumbers, talking to her while she is frying the tacos… my mouth already watering because something delicious is about to be tasted.

Fried Tacos

Ingredients:

12 corn tortillas

2 chicken breasts

1 lettuce

1 cucumber

2 tomatoes

1 red onion

Mexican salsa

sour cream

Method:

Boil the chicken breasts and cut them in large thick pieces. Put some chicken in the middle of a tortilla and fold the tortilla and fry it in a pan with oil. Slice the lettuce, cucumbers, tomatoes, and onion.

Mexican Salsa:

1 can of chopped tomatoes

2 chilli chipotles

1 clove of garlic

salt black pepper and oregano

Blend all the ingredients. Put the tacos in a plate, cover them with the salad and put some salsa on top of everything and some sour cream on the top.

French Toast

Colm Keegan

For best results, your first experience of French toast should be when watching the film Kramer vs. Kramer, the old movie that depicts the break-up of a family. Ideally, you should be about five years of age or so, with your own parents already split up. When Dustin Hoffman tries to make everything alright for his small son by cooking French toast and it ends in tears, you should feel bad for them both, and somehow for yourself.

Leave the memory to steep in your subconscious, along with things like your first kiss, or the first time you felt grass tickle the soles of your feet. Let it sit until you don't even know it's there. Then, when a friend cooks French toast with maple syrup for you in his beautiful new country home, you should get impressed by the woody surroundings and the glorious conservatory instead of making any connections. When you take the recipe home you should hardly recognise its worth.

Leave the memory in the dark. Cook French toast in your own home over and over for the next few years through the humble trials and traumas of your budding family's life. Replace maple syrup with light sprinklings of sugar, because you're the only one who really likes it anyway. Stop having children after your third daughter and let your family mature. Buy a trampoline; lose buddies while building firm friendships, keep buying a bigger car. Fall in and out of love with your partner and yourself - repeat. For best results, occasionally search your life for meaning, sometimes finding none. Scatter old selves like used crusts through the past, pepper your life with mistakes. Accumulate some small kernels of truth, you'll need them over and over as you go.

When your middle daughter shakes you awake on a Sunday morning, preferably one of those Sundays where you're hung-over or just can't deal with getting up, understand her pleas for French toast for what they actually are. Stand up straight and slide on your slippers. Stumble blinking into the kitchen. Guzzle orange juice while standing over the pan. Smile when your three-year-old climbs up on the counter and maybe let her use the whisk to beat the eggs. Listen to your thirteen year old come out of her room like clockwork because she knows what's cooking. Dish it up. Give your partner hers in bed, share a smile but leave her be - she deserves the rest.

Finally, watch the children flit in and out of the kitchen to bounce on the trampoline in the sunshine. Sit with a cup of tea and your favourite book on the history of the world, one with maps whose borders ebb and flow over the ages like the tides, remember how meaningless all that far away stuff is. Do all these things, just so, and deep down inside something dings.

French Toast

Ingredients:

4 eggs

6 slices of bread

A little milk

pinch of salt

sugar or maple syrup

butter for frying

Method:

Break eggs into a bowl. Add a drop of milk and a pinch of salt. Cut bread into halves.

Heat pan to medium heat and melt butter. Dip bread in egg and fry until lightly browned.

Serve with sprinklings of sugar or maple syrup.

Two Tribes

Nyamwenda Massamba

I am from the north of Tanzania, Musoma, Mara region, which is located at Lake Victoria, East Africa. I came to Ireland October 1999 to study. I am a qualified Community Development Officer, I worked in Tanzania for eleven years and I am currently working in Dublin, Ireland as a Community Development officer with An Cosan, Jobstown, Tallaght. I am coordinating Education Programmes for young mothers from ethnic minority backgrounds ranging in ages 14-24 years.

My parents are both from North of Tanzania and from different tribes. I have experienced great learning from both. My father is from the Ruri tribe, they are based in Kurwaki, Mugango, Musoma Rural. The majority of the people who live in Kurwaki village are fishermen and my father's family have been involved in fishing when they were young but changed career after finishing school.

My mother she is from the Zanaki tribe, Bunda district in Mara region. Zanaki people love to eat meat. There is a joke about this tribe that, because they loved meat so much, somebody decided to play with their mind and was successful. This is what was told them, to get more meat you have to plant/grow the bulls. If you pick healthy bulls and plant them after a certain period of time they will grow and also, not to forget to water the place. So they did and nothing came out and they lost.

I am delighted to share a story about my favorite food (Tanzania), my mother's favorite food and my father's favorite food, pilau.

When it is cooked in any country the smell reminds me of Tanzania. Pilau is a favorite Tanzanian rice dish, cooked during ceremonies; weddings, birthdays, at Christmas and other special occasions. Pilau has a very unique taste, the recipes can differ slightly because of different creative ways of cooking but the delicious smell is the same. Tanzania Pilau is traditionally cooked with chicken or beef, I prefer to use chicken and then serve the dish with a simple chicken stew or salad/kachumbali. For vegetarian you just take out beef or chicken and use the spices. What makes Tanzanin Pilau very special is the smell of different spices and garlic. I remember the first time I ate pilau, it was prepared by my mother. The whole house was a smell of spices, I was very happy because people around us knew something special was happening in our house. Traditionally when you have cooked pilau you have to share with your neighbours by putting some on a plate and sending it to their houses.

Zanaki tribe (my mother) -This is the best food I had when I went to visit my grandparents on my mother's side. My grandfather was a farmer, with his own cattle, and also a butcher supplying meat to the community and secondary schools around. What I liked most was before he sold the meat we had to select what type of meat we would love to eat. My favorite food was dried meat – a very nice fillet was selected and dried by sun's rays for a few days until it was ready. Then the meat was boiled until soft and then put on a pan with oil, onions, tomatoes, spinach, and milk cream. The cooked meat with spinach has to go with ugali (stiff porridge) from millet and cassava flour. The good thing about dried meat is that it can be kept for as long as required because when it is dry it is very hard like a piece of wood and before cooking it needs to be soaked. The dried meat is known as 'kimoro' and stiff porridge in Zanaki is 'ubukima', in Swahili it is known as 'ugali'. This food can be eaten at lunch time or dinner.

Ruri tribe (my father) – My father is from the lake side of a place called Kurwaki, Musoma Rural. The majority there are fishermen and even women know how to catch fish. My favorite food from my father's tribe is small fish they call them "furu" cooked with onions, bush tomatoes (we call them bush tomatoes because they grow in the bush) especially around the lake and the small fish will be cooked in the special pot made locally by women using clay. I enjoy most when the small fish are served with sweet potatoes but also you can eat with ugali.

Tanzanian Pilau

Ingredients:

1 cup basmati oil

2 tbsp olive oil

¼ cup onions

1 tbsp crushed garlic

1 tsp pilau masala

2 to 3 cups chicken broth (boiling)

½ cup coconut milk (canned)

big potato

salt

Method:

Put oil in a pot, heat on medium setting. Add pieces of potatoes, stir until the colour is brown, add rice and onions. Stir until the translucent colour of the rice starts to turn white. Add garlic and pilau masala, cinnamon, black pepper, cardamom. Keep stirring until the garlic is cooked. In a separate bowl, mix the coconut milk with ½ cup of chicken broth. Add the coconut mixture to the rice. Cover the pot and turn heat to the lowest settings. Add chicken broth ½ cup at a time to the rice until it is cooked.

Coconut milk is optional.

Flavours of Home

Family Recipe

Eloubou

Aimee Tshibasu

I am from The Democratic Republic of Congo. I choose this recipe because I miss my country and because it is my husband's best food. In my language we call it "Eloubou".

Roasted Potatoes

Ingredients:

potatoes

salt

vegetable oil

chicken cube

Method:

Boil the potatoes (un-skinned) with the water, salt and the chicken cube. When the potatoes are ready, remove them from the water and let them dry up and then fry them in hot vegetable oil. When the potatoes look roasted, remove them from the oil and they are ready to serve.

Gathering Leaves

Ambroise Isamala

This is a true story of my family and the manner in which my mother prepared food and our favourite recipes.

I was born into a family of eight children. I am the eldest and I have two brothers and five sisters. Our mother made a recipe called "Leaves of Manioc" in which she put aubergine, olive oil or palm oil and those leaves were accompanied by a 'paquet' of grilled fish or salt fish or meat. That meal was a favourite for everybody and all and one came to eat with us around the camp fire. These were large corn leaves, which grew wild, gathered in the nearby fields. I loved this food and still remember eating it. It is very much part of my Congolese heritage.

My father died 20 years ago. He loved eating chikwangue (cassava flour) with manioc leaves, (cassava vegetables). He also loved paquet, a fish meat. Paquet was his favourite meal. There was also a kind of chickwangue with corn that we called "Mpó", that I also really loved. About the "foufou", my father loved one with a mix of flour and corn. For breakfast my mother made a sort of doughnut in which she mixed corn beef or pork. My mother woke up very early in the morning, around three o'clock so that everything was ready before we went to school. She was a school teacher. Those doughnuts were succulent. So much so that my brother who is now a professor burned his bottom three times while eating it outside when he sat on the hot stones which were used for cooking.

Pondu, Leaves of Manioc

Ingredients:

leaves of manioc

aubergine

olive oil/palm oil

paquet of grilled fish

salt fish or meat

The Grieving Process

Graham Carry

I remember when I was about ten years old I had just gotten a new bicycle and decided to cycle to my grandmother's to see her and to show her the bicycle. She was my paternal grandmother and there were twelve children in my dad's family. Granddad had passed away a short time earlier. He used to grow his own vegetables and had a greenhouse that he built himself.

When I got to my grandmother's, I went down the side of the house and straight into the back garden. The vegetable patch was over-grown and the cauliflower leaves were full of holes from being eaten away by insects. The greenhouse was full of really red tomatoes and a small few green strawberries.

I went into the kitchen where my grandmother was cooking soup and brown bread. She cut me a slice and put a big blob of butter on the bread. It was lovely. She gave me a bowl of soup and had one herself. We sat down at the table to eat. I was watching her and I could not believe the amount of pepper she put in her soup, she just kept shaking it in. She asked me would I like to try some. I said "no thank you Nan!" I stayed with her for a while and we went out to the garden and tidied up the vegetable plot and dug up the cauliflowers.

I went home after a while and thanked Nan for the soup and said I would drop down again soon. Looking back, I can see how Nan, as well as the garden, was affected by the grieving process.

Graham's Granny's Brown Bread

Ingredients:

1 ½ mugs of coarse whole wheat flour

½ mug of oat flakes (porridge)

½ mug of all-bran

1 egg

pint of buttermilk/sour mild (normal milk is also okay)

tsp of bread soda

pinch of salt

Method:

Put all the ingredients into a large bowl. Mix together very well, heat oven to 200?. Grease a loaf tin and place mix in tin, then place in the oven. Cook for 40 minutes or so. To check if the bread is cooked, you can push on top of the bread, if firm, the bread is cooked. Put the knife into the middle of the bread and if the knife comes out relatively dry, the bread is ready.

A Mighty Brew

Joan Power

They say you can't live on love, but in the spring of nineteen seventy five when I married my hero, we came close. Food didn't matter. Parties did. *Unsupervised-by-parents-and-buckets-of-booze-type parties*. In a rented flat in the cheaper part of Dublin City, we were officially grown up and, finally, the authors of our own misfortune.

"That's not a very desirable area, you know," my worried father had advised.

I was airily dismissive.

"Oh Dad, we can save lots for a house and I'm safe with Sam".

My new husband had proved himself a courageous protector on several occasions. I had no forewarning of his Achilles' heel.

One cold March evening, armed with our friend's recipe for home brewed beer, we made five gallons of the stuff for our first married 'knees-up'.

Jim and Bernie Mills's recipe was the stuff of legend. A mighty brew not for the fainthearted, its effects were spoken of with awe. Even as a shandy (with lemonade), it could floor roomfuls of people. This circumstance was considered the true mark of a great party. The ingredients were cheap and accessible, though the process was slow and required patience. Bottling could not be done before fermentation was completed. There was good reason for this but I didn't ask it. I too had an Achilles' heel; impatience.

In the steamy kitchen I boiled, mixed and stirred the dung-coloured dried hops with water and sugar. Sam washed forty glass bottles. We sang as we worked; '*Goodbye Ruby Tuesday.*' The smell was appalling, visceral and acrid with malty undertones. The giant white plastic bin was stowed under the kitchen table. Each day a glass barometer was dropped in to check the progress of fermentation. It was a messy business but forty pints of beer for an outlay of four pounds? Oh yes, you can live on love.

My father, on his visits, viewed the proceedings silently.

For weeks, I fretted at the barometer. It bobbed in the noxious liquid far from the red mark which signaled the end of fermentation. Ignoring Sam's protests, I 'bottled.'

Proudly I stashed my ranks of amber soldiers in a normally unused cupboard. Mice invaded this corner cupboard through ancient pipes, disdaining my traps. But sealed bottles, I reasoned, were mouse-proof. Also the wind-chill factor in this cupboard would keep the beer beautifully cold. I drifted off to sleep that night mentally drawing up my guest list.

In the depths of the night we were brutally ripped from slumber by explosive gunshots. I gripped Sam in terror. Dad was right, this was a dodgy neighbourhood. People were being shot! We clung together as a cacophony of cracks and explosions followed on each other like fireworks. Finally all was silent.

"Stay here and don't come out," Sam commanded sternly.

I heard him switch on the kitchen light. I heard a horrible wail and then, with a blood-freezing yell, he torpedoed back into the bedroom and launched himself at me.

"It's mayhem out there! I told you it was too soon to bottle the beer, it was still fermenting. The bottles have exploded inside the cupboard, blowing those god-damned mice to kingdom-come! There's beer and blood and…and…MOUSE BODIES. But oh Susie, there's *movement*, some of them are still alive! Oh, Susie!"I stared in disbelief at my Goliath, wild-eyed and petrified.

"Stay here and don't come out," I commanded sternly.

The battlefield presented only the dead. The living had staggered home. As I came to terms with my shattered kitchen, I was struck by the expression on the face of one of the victims. Sprawled drunkenly, its tiny pink paws splayed outwards in crucified gratitude, it was comically akin to our often inebriated landlord.

A quivering Sam did not see the joke.

Ah well, marriage is a delicate mixture, with rich and diverse ingredients. Achilles plastered over his heel and I practiced patience. And we never screwed the lid too tight on any fermenting passions. It was a mighty brew and a lasting recipe.

Ingredients:

1 Home Brew Beer Kit

2 young newly weds

8 – 10   live mice

2 Achilles' heels

40 glass bottles

Масленица (Maslenitsa)

Maria Petrovicheva McManus

I remember coming back home after long summer days (we used to spend most of our time outside). I would feel quite tired and very hungry after spending most of the day outdoors. So, the first question on my mind was: "What's for dinner"? When I sneaked into the kitchen to find the answer I'd see Mom mixing milk and four in the bowl and think "Pancakes". I would stay nearby to grab the first one. After I got it, I would go back into the living room to watch TV.

In my family there are four people, so my mom always made sure that everybody had enough to eat. In the case of pancakes there were plenty of them. After a big meal everybody would get together to spend the rest of the evening watching TV, and there was no better way of doing it than in Mom's arms, full of that lovely warm smell of love, care and...pancakes!

In Russia, we have a pancake week (about five weeks before Easter). Originally, this holiday represented the new beginning – "Say goodbye to winter and hello to sprint". The pancake itself was the symbol of sun (warm, round, yellow). Each day of the week had its own meaning. For example, on Monday, the first pancake was given away to poor people with the words 'Please eat this pancake and pray for the souls of those who died". And there was a day allocated especially to 'meet the parents'. The families of young people planned weddings for later on that year (usually towards the end of August, September and October, when there is more fresh food than ever in the year). The week has the name – Масленица (maslenitsa)

Pancakes

Ingredients:

1 ltr of milk,

½ cup sunflower oil

A little bit of salt

½ tsp baking soda

2 medium eggs

½ cup sugar

4 cups plain flour

Method:

Into a big enough bowl pour the milk, add salt, baking powder, 2 eggs. Start mixing it. While mixing, add sugar and gradually add flour, add oil afterwards. Only use hot frying pan, pour some of the mix (enough for 1 pancake) in the middle of the pan and turn it to spread the mix to get thin and large pancakes. Leave it for about 20-25 seconds. From start to finish, it will take about 30 minutes. If your milk has gone off – the solution is not to worry! You can use that milk to make pancakes.

If there are too many pancakes, lots of them are left over then the solution again is not to worry. You can make different fillings and wrap them with pancakes (my favourite is mince fried with finely chopped onions). You can add finely chopped boiled egg to it as well. Wrap two tablespoons of the filling in a pancake, put them in the fridge. Take them out as they are needed and fry them lightly on each side for a couple of minutes. They are tasty - and make a quick snack, or, depending on the amount – dinner.

A Big Pizza Pie

Niamh Bagnell

My mother invented Pizza. In my world at least, she introduced the original pizza pie way before pizzas came frozen in boxes, or from the fleece lined square bags on the backs of motorbikes. It was even before the turtles had blasted onto 'The Den', in the mid-'80', addicted to their runny pizza, thin crusts and all.

My mother's pizza was different though. I suppose it still is. From my earliest memories of dinner parties, the ones I'd try and stay awake for, then fall asleep, to be later woken late at night by the laughter downstairs, she would have the pizza as her centre piece. I'd come down in my one- piece fluffy pyjamas, dopey with sleep but excited by the visitors, and there it would be – the aroma lusciously draped around the room, tomatoey napkins left on plates, adults looking satisfied on their seats. A mysterious huge hot pie, alive with salty tastefulness, with broiling hot filling, thickly sliced up juicy rashers, too big for one bite. It was a hit, and one of the first things I ever remember someone begging for the recipe.

I only got to taste it when I was finally judged big enough to appreciate the contents. The thick layer of chewy cheddar toasted on top – the secret cheddar hidden within the crumbly pastry that formed the base, contributed to the weightiness and decadence of the meal. It was a serious meal all on its own, a proper dinner. It doesn't compare to the Domino's, Goodfella's or the thin, crusty, runny American pizzas, which are all great in their way. It's a pizza from a parallel universe – an entirely different spin on what could be done with pastry, tomato and cheese, and I loved it.

Way back in 1978, the ICA around east cork were doing demonstrations of this recipe at their gatherings. This is where my mother says she learned it. I was born in 1979...

My dad loved it too.

For the Pie Crust:

Combine 12 oz flour, 3 oz margarine, a teaspoon of mustard, a teaspoon of mixed herbs, 1 egg, 2 oz of grated cheese and 6-8 tablespoons of milk.

The pie crust is to be kneaded – do not use a rolling pin. Then lay into the desired tray. Prick the base with a fork while heating to aerate. Cook at 200 C for 10 -12 minutes or until the pastry base is set.

For the Sauce:

Fry up an onion, chopped in 1cm cubes in oil. Add Mushrooms and Bacon slices and lightly fry. (Either use lardons (rasher cubes) or slice rashers in 1 inch wide strips. Add 1 Teaspoon of oregano, 2 teaspoons of tomato puree and 1 tin of tomatoes, add 1 teaspoon of corn flour to thicken. Bring to the boil – allow to simmer for 10 minutes before adding into the pastry tray.

For the Cheese:

Grate loads – and I mean LOADS of cheese. Cover the surface of the pie completely with it, cook for 16 minutes at 200 C. Warn people that 5 minutes of blowing on it might be advisable.

Written in Gold

David Mohan

My Italian aunt was no cook. Her sisters would make *Lobster Pasquale*, elaborate casseroles, *Osso Buco*, their own pannacotta from scratch even, planning feasts where pots would simmer all day whilst they chopped vegetables or laid sheets of gelatine. But she preferred time spent with her cats, a pillow lodged in the arch of her back, a constant Sudoku puzzle or detective novel at hand. When she did cook, it was crankily, slamming metal down, chopping with an aggressive flick. She reserved the most love for her cat's food – cooking them chicken, even going so far as to buy them delicacies like cuttlefish which they sniffed at bemusedly.

It was for this reason I developed a love for piadinas, for gelato on-the-street, for on-the-hop restaurant ravioli, and most of all for the Italian patisserie. After work, Giancarlo would meet me and we would walk across *Duomo* piazza, through the arcade, past *La Scala* and down the little network of streets that lead to the *Academi Di Belle Arti Di Brera* and the student quarter. The patisseries down *Via Dante* were too expensive, and as they were for tourists, too inauthentic.

The student quarter was where you found the good, cheap eats. The modest looking facades to restaurants where locals ate, not tourists. And the homelier patisseries, run like bakeries, that were less an adornment than an aspect of a district's personal flavour. The one run on *Via Spezia* was the one we went to most. It had a bench outside, for people to sit on a summer evening, facing a laneway, and eat some pastry out of a tissue package.

The Italian patisserie is not like the French – it has not quite the same elaborate repertoire, nor the same intricate artfulness. Its food looks plain mostly - the sweet things dusted with icing sugar, the savoury with flour. For this reason it was approachable enough to become a haunt.

In those days, they sold panettone cake, something Giancarlo would bring to my family as a gift at Christmas. They had their version of the Austrian Sacher Torte, and little choux cakes like ellipses to the éclairs exclamation mark, filled with chocolate, coffee and vanilla creams. They had miniature fruit tarts lathered with gelatine so the berries always shone dewy fresh. And ranks of beloved mini-pastries - a hybrid cross between mignon and biscotti - the sorts of tiny biscuit sculptures to adorn the rim of an espresso. They had unexpected extravagances too - bulbous conchs abrim with fruit candied cream, sinister glazed cakes candied with black cherries like fish eyes.

I would come here alone as often as not, when Giancarlo was at work and 'Mama' Anna Lisa in a temper. It was a home away from the suburbs, a place that felt metropolitan and glamorous. Rozzano was fine as far as it went, and exotic in its own way, with its pastel painted cooperative apartment blocks and graffitied skateboarding park. But I felt closer to feeling foreign, to being at the edge of things in somewhere slightly anonymous, with just a hint of the international about it.

I could read or watch people for as long as I wanted, committed only to buying a fresh cappuccino on the hour. Sometimes I would read *Il Giorno* for practise, and sometimes, sneak glances into the kitchen. The cooks would be red-faced, shouting usually, their hands sometimes white to the elbows. They and I had lives, secret from another, from the words in our heads to how their hands rose up in the air to conduct a point whilst mine rested on the table, fidgeting with a pen.

Some moments, often the most inconsequential ones, are written in gold in the mind, for whatever reason. For me, my abiding Italian memory is of a late autumn evening, rain splashed on the glass, the street darkening and throwing up lights in smears, the sputter of froth in a milk jug, the scent of chocolate and perfume, the clatter of trays in the kitchen, the last gust of steam from the oven from the last batch cooked, ceramic plates and saucers clashed against glass counters, the homeless man who would come in at the last hour raising his voice to receive a paper bag of leftover broken biscuits, (the way he would cast me a quick glance, as though he recognised me), the crumpled serviettes, the crumbs left on each table like a sputtered code, the way the day was swept brusquely up from under feet and into bags and knotted and put away, the way I would, at the unspoken sign of the lights flickering - the spotlight of the last table left in its own little circle - the way I would walk out into the cold night finally, the reddish stone of the street looking quaint and cut straight from the 60s, and because I was in love, feel, just for that moment, that the taste of the rain on my lips was sweet.

Cannoli

Ingredients:

1 15-ounce carton ricotta cheese
3/4 cup powdered sugar 3/4 cup powdered sugar
1 tsp vanilla
1 ounce bittersweet or semisweet chocolate, grated
4 ounces bittersweet or semisweet chocolate, chopped
1 tablespoon shortening
12 to 14 purchased cannoli shells
3/4 cup finely chopped pistachio nuts
1 cup whipping cream

Method:

For filling, in a medium bowl, stir together ricotta cheese, powdered sugar, and vanilla until almost smooth. Stir in 1 ounce bittersweet chocolate. Cover and chill up to 6 hours. Meanwhile, in a small saucepan, heat and stir 4 ounces bittersweet chocolate and the shortening over low heat until melted. Remove from heat. Transfer to a small bowl. Dip both ends of the cannoli shells in chocolate, letting excess drip off. Sprinkle chocolate ends with pistachio nuts. Place on a wire rack placed over waxed paper to dry (about 45 minutes). When chocolate is dry, in a medium bowl, beat whipping cream at medium speed of an electric mixer or with a wire whisk until stiff peaks form. Fold into the ricotta mixture. Spoon filling into a decorating bag fitted with a large round or open star tip (or spoon into a resealable plastic bag; seal bag. Snip off a small corner of the bag). Pipe filling into shells. Cover and chill up to 2 hours. Makes 12 servings.

Chocolate Cannoli:

Prepare Cannoli as directed, except stir 1/4 cup unsweetened cocoa powder in with the ricotta cheese.

Flavours of Home

Family Memory

_____

_____

_____

_____

_____

_____

_____

_____

_____

_____

_____

_____

_____

_____

The Breakfast

Abdullahi Osman El-Tom

It must be around ten 0'clock because my dad wants me to get the breakfast ready. I know it is around ten 0'clock because my dad's radio fades away around this time and I can see him struggling to re-tune it. Most radios in Broosh don't work well when it is too hot and they go funny until late afternoon. My dad gets frustrated and he turns it off and says it is breakfast time and that makes me hungry. I love serving breakfast because it is one of my most important duties of the day and I will be free after that to go wherever I want. My duty is simple and clear and I know it well. I have to bring out a large dish of porridge into the shop veranda, which is attached to the house wall. I also have to bring out a jug of drinking water and it has to be from the coldest water pot in the house because the weather is hot. And I don't forget to fill up the water vessel and bring a bar of soap for washing hands. The bar of soap is a joke, not because it is so small that you cannot hold it well in your hands, although that is true. Rather, it is because it is rarely used and still my dad gives out to me if it is not there. If anybody asks for the soap, you can be sure it is after eating and not before when the hands are really dirty.

We are now ready to eat. We all squat around the dish, my dad, my brother, myself and two shoppers whose names I don't know. Any customer who happens to be in the shop when breakfast is eaten is invited to join. My dad says the whole purpose of eating in the shop is to welcome strangers to share the food with us. It is only mean people who hide in their houses when they take their meals and we are not like those. My dad always repeats what Prophet Mohammed said and I know it by word: "The more hands are sharing the food, the more blessed it is". The saying sounds funny because it is real Arabic and that is different from how we speak in Broosh. Sometimes when my dad talks like that I say "Is that Koran dad?" and he says "No son, this is a prophetic speech". Sometimes he talks like that and I ask him and he gets amused and says "No, idiot. This is poetry, not Koran" and everybody around us laughs at me but I don't care. He is only joking and I know he doesn't think I am a real idiot.

We are now sitting around the dish waiting for a signal to start eating. It seems like hours and hours and everybody looks hungry. We are not allowed to touch the food before it is blessed by the most senior in the company. You have to be ancient to be allowed to do that and that is why my older brother cannot do it either. It is not my dad who is going to do it today but an old man sitting next to me. If you could see his face and the way he breathes, you think he is going to drop dead right now and we will never be able to taste the food. You cannot eat with somebody just dead next to you, can you? The old man looks scruffy and a bit dirty but there is something special and rather powerful in him. He looks like somebody who is full of knowledge and wisdom. His hands are dirty and full of cracks but when I offered him the bar of soap earlier, he looked at me and said "Thank you Grandson, I don't need that". He is so gentle and I didn't feel bad when he rejected my offer. He actually made me feel like his real grandson when he said it. My dad now looks at him and says "Bless the food for us Hajii". The old stranger stretches his right hand fingers and places them on the tip of the heaped porridge and says "In the name of Allah, the Merciful, the Compassionate. May Allah, the Almighty, bless this food".

"Amen" we all respond and descend like vultures on the dish.

Oh the breakfast that day is so delicious. The dish is so huge and has at least two kilograms of millet porridge and look at it now! Well, it is empty now. The porridge is so carefully shaped in a half-ball shape, with the round bit on the top and is surrounded by thick sauce. It is my favourite sauce made of yoghurt and has all the goodies in it; sun-dried meat, tomatoes, okra, butter and onion. The hot chillies are just right and we don't have to drink too much water to cool it down. Within a few minutes, we run short of sauce and I have to dash into the house and get more. Fortunately, there is some more available. On some days, and when extra customers appear from nowhere, we run short of food. Nobody bothers and they just say "Blessed is what we had" and my mom doesn't have to start cooking all over again. I know that my mom gets embarrassed when there is not enough food for all but there is no way around it. There is surplus food on most days but sometimes there is not enough and these are passing guests who are in a rush and cannot wait for extra food to be prepared. I cannot blame them for they have a long way to go and their donkeys are loaded with water and waiting for them in front of the shop. My mom says 'These are Allah's guests and only He knows how many of them will be there for breakfast. You plan for two and you get five and you plan for six and you get none".

"What are you going to do today, Saeed?" My dad says.

"I don't know. Maybe I go to my friend Mohammed and we go out for a walk".

"Don't go too far away. Never further than the first fields nearby and certainly nowhere near the wells, and no climbing rocks either", my dad says.

"That is okay dad" I say.

"Remember to take the donkey to the water centre this evening. This is its watering day and it must be very thirsty", he adds.

My brother looks at me and he is full of himself. He doesn't have to be told what to do because he is a senior intermediate boy and he thinks he is older and wiser and is always away from troubles. He notices that I don't appreciate his smile but he says nothing for a while. He waits for further instructions from my dad and when nothing comes, he says:

"take the empty dish back home before you disappear, and when you are out, stay away from mouse holes. There might be snakes inside them".

I resent his pompous advice but I say nothing, just in case my dad supports him and he gets bossier.

The clearance of the breakfast debris doesn't take long and I am now in the shop doing my best to help. My dad and my brother are busy with some customers. They both seem to be doing more talks and jokes than work. Who cares about a stupid bunch of goats that lost their way home for a while and are now found safe but are very thirsty? That is what they are talking about and, believe it or not, they look interested and even manage to make jokes out of that. Do I give a damn if they are stolen or eaten by a wolf?

I may be young but I can still be useful in the shop and help my brother who thinks he is the manager. I stack some cigarette boxes on the shelf making sure that the two types are piled separate. Here are the smelly ones called 'Abu Nakhala' and they have a picture of palm trees on the box. These are the cheap cigarettes that have no filters and they are popular among people with little or no money. On the other side I put Embassy cigarettes. They have filters and they are bought by smart people like government people, teachers and truck drivers. My magnificent artistic construction is nearly complete on the shelf when disaster hits. A stupid spider appears from nowhere, making me jump, and the cigarette boxes fall and scatter everywhere on the floor. My dad who is talking to a customer is now furious. He doesn't see the spider and will not take that as an excuse for the mess either:

"Get out and play outside the shop", he roars.

My brother is amused and is too mean to blame the spider. He doesn't even correct my dad and tell him that I am helping and not playing in the shop. He cannot stop laughing at me while sweeping the boxes back on the shelf:

"Only a spider. Not even a scorpion", my brother says with a dirty grin.

I leave the shop feeling humiliated but cannot think of any defence. That shop is full of spiders and if you add other insects and creatures like flies, cockroaches, beetles, geckos and other crawlies that don't even have names, you'd think my dad trades in them. There are more of them put together than goods in this shop. I don't need to think about that and I will never try to help them again because I have better things to do.

I can see my friend Mohammed coming looking for me. He is right in the open space where other shops are. The shops are arranged forming a square and there is an open space for peddlers who use it for trading on Wednesdays. That is where I will meet my friend before my dad thinks about sending me to fetch out something. Mohammed is still only a few yards away from his father's shop which is slightly smaller than our shop. Mohammed's family shop is not like ours in another way also.   It is built of grass like all other shops in Broosh and ours is the only one that is made of sun-baked bricks. But they all have crawlies like ours and they don't seem to bother about them. You could get everything the villagers need in these shops and sometimes they sell exactly the same goods for exactly the same price.

Extracted from *Growing up in Darfur, Sudan* (The Sudanese Studies Centre, 2007)

By Abdullahi Osman El-Tom, Senior Lecturer of Anthropology

at the National University of Ireland, Maynooth.

Silk

Eileen Cordial

The street *w*here I lived as a child was lined on either side with identical two-up, two-down council houses. At equally spaced intervals, telegraph poles towered like totems and on those wires sat a symphony of birds strung out like sheet music. Together with Donal Abu on RTE radio, that chorus made up those early morning sounds.

In as far as weather permitted, most of the front doors of the houses were left open and as the hallways were very small, it was possible to see into the kitchens of these houses. Each tableau in this domestic gallery presented much the same image, families sat around the table in kitchens which also doubled as sitting rooms. Depending on the employment scene, men were often stood like sentries at garden gates, aimlessly looking up and down, perhaps expecting some mythical messenger to appear at any moment with news of work. Before going back indoors again an obligatory spit landed in the road, as if a javelin throwing contest was in progress between the men.

Most of the social 'action' in the street was played out visiting neighbours and sitting around those tables chatting and sharing news. One house in the street was the most popular and had 'open house' most of the time. The characters living in that house were just so witty, always having a quirky 'handle' on life and all the latest gossip. They weren't averse to a drop of cider either and more than the odd woodbine cigarette. Had these people lived in different times and in different circumstances, they would have had salons and had the ear of Rousseau or Voltaire – definitely! The matriarch in this house even looked a little like Marie Antoinette, with her white hair piled high in spiralling curls. She had a navyish tinge to her skin, a blood condition no doubt. The neighbours right next door to me kept a donkey (for drawing turf from the bog) in the fields behind the back gardens. His braying was also part of the acoustics of my childhood.

My father was a postman and wore a big black uniform with heavy brass buttons. He looked like a big black bird himself, the peak of his hat as glossy as a blackbird's beak. My mother came from Galway and often sang *The Galway Shawl* while she worked. She loved Ceili music too, The Kilfenora Ceili Band from Clare being her favourite. She always had the radio on, her hands, whatever task they were engaged with, moving in rhythm with the music. At night my older brothers and sisters would listen to pop songs on Radio Luxemburg or Radio Caroline.

Bread making was very much a part of family ritual. Truth to tell my mother never used weighing scales. A handful of this, a fistful of that. It was a knack, the same way an artist knows how to gauge perspective. Her measuring utensils were the bowl of her hands and a very accurate eye. With lightning speed she'd whip out the red basin kept in the scullery and have all the ingredients harmonised before you could say 'hot soda bread'. Her hands were the hands of a countrywoman, roughened from daily hand washing and the weather. She liked the feel of the flour on her skin. It was like 'talcum powder'.

Sometimes we sat around our own table eating soda bread with currants, a treat which was served on a fairly regular basis. Depending on the number of currants we joked that it was 'a railway cake' with a currant at every station. Or, my father, being a postman, might say the number was equal to the amount of letters from America that particular week. It didn't take a Colombo or Sherlock Holmes to figure out the reason why. Most of the young people in the street emigrated to England rather than the states at that time. As I was a teenager then, I often secretly counted out 'he loves me, he loves me not'. The taste of that counting was like velvet on my tongue.

One day, as we were eating our soda bread with currants, a burning smell drifted up through the back garden and swirled its way like a fog around us. It was end of summer, too early for bonfires. We wondered what could possibly be the cause and ran upstairs to look out the back bedroom window. There was indeed a pyre billowing out smoke and fragments of old newspapers and household goods no longer deemed worth keeping. It turned out that the daughter of the house next door took the opportunity of indiscriminately 'clearing out' when her parents were absent, the clearing process extending to her mother's silk wedding dress, lovingly folded in tissue and kept in the airing cupboard beside the range for thirty years. The Kilfenora Ceili Band was turned up more than an octave or two that day to tune out the commotion that ensued.

Soda Bread with Currants is: The glow of a red basis like a fire lighting the kitchen, the white powder on my mother's hands, open doors, the smell of a fiddle burning out 'The Galway Shawl', the touch of silken ashes at end of summer.

Ingredients:

2 cups sifted all-purpose flour

2 tbsp sugar

2 tsp baking powder

½ tsp salt

¼ tsp baking soda

1 cup currants

1 cup buttermilk

butter

Method:

Into a medium mixing bowl sift together the flour, sugar, baking powder, salt and soda. Stir in currants, then stir in the buttermilk, stirring just until mixture is blended. Turn out onto a lightly floured surface and knead about eight times. Shape into a six inch round. Place on an un-greased baking sheet. Cut a cross on the top of the loaf. Bake at 375 degrees for 40 minutes or until golden brown. Brush hot soda bread with butter. Break apart or slice. Serve warm.

Flavours of Home

Family Recipe

_____

_____

_____

_____

_____

_____

_____

_____

_____

_____

_____

_____

_____

_____

A Small Tyranny

Brian Kirk

Imagine a boy, a small boy of four or five, the youngest in a large family. Imagine this boy, doted on by his parents and older siblings, a boy who can do no wrong, cosseted from the world, a boy who knows only love and security. Imagine a young life blessed by good health and fond companionship in a shambling old house by the railway line, an island fitted snug in the folds between two small towns, blissfully ignorant of all prevailing venal cares. Imagine a childish idyll if you will.

And now imagine dinner times in that old house. We Irish make no claims to be gourmands or gourmets, but my mother was an able cook. Sunday was roast chicken, Monday soup made from the bones, Tuesday sausages and beans, Wednesday mince and gravy, Thursday pork chops, Friday fish and Saturday the unhelpfully named meat soup. All served, of course, with potatoes of one sort or another. On Sundays I refused to eat. On Mondays, not a morsel passed my mouth. On Tuesdays and Thursdays I would not lift a fork. On Fridays I maintained my fast. On Saturdays I sullenly watched as an oily film formed upon the surface of my untouched soup. Only on Wednesdays did I eat greedily with spoon and fork my mince and gravy mixed with mashed potato.

How did I live back then? All week I scoffed the thickly buttered heels of homemade wheaten bread or snacked on stolen biscuits while my mother was diverted by her never ending chores. I am a bloody fool. How did I live...with myself? All week I acted like a spoiled brat, a boy who cared nothing for his poor mother's feelings. I sat before her with creased lips firmly shut, arms folded, unbreakable, unflinching. For a while she scolded, then she begged, next she screamed. Eventually, she cried. I remained aloof however. Little by little I ground her down, and so began the small tyranny of mince and gravy.

A short time after a neighbour came to take care of us while my mother was in hospital. I felt that flutter of confused impatience that comes with potential loss for the first time in my young life and began to regret my behaviour. In an effort to keep my spirits up, the surrogate cooked mince and gravy, but when I sat down to eat I was appalled. Onions! The tyranny continued. One day soon after my mother came home I could tell by the way she quickly left my plate before me and disappeared that something was not right. It looked alright, if a little darker than was normal. Oh, but the taste, the foul taste, sour and spicy all at once! I called to her "this is not right, this is not mince!" but she was adamant. She'd had to use a different butcher she said, that was all. I stood my ground. I wore her down until she cried, admitting she had lied, that it was actually black pudding and mince. I pushed my untouched plate away, hurt but vindicated and left her sobbing.

Imagine a small tyranny persisting for a year perhaps, and I a little Hitler casually imposing my will without care for consequence. Imagine being that person now, remembering these things years later, regretting the pain I caused her, looking at my own kids when they refuse to eat, feeling empathy at last, a parent's raw emotion, and a bad taste in my mouth.

Ol' Fashioned Free Range Kids

Valerie O'Brien

In the 'sixties five of us kids would visit granny every Saturday. We travelled one and a half to two hours, each way, unaccompanied, by bus, from Ballyfermot, ("bally-far-out", Granny would say), to Kimmage, changing busses at Christ Church Cathedral. Usually, we travelled in twos or threes and sometimes alone. We ranged in age from six to ten years. On fine days, half- way, we'd spend our bus fare on sweets and walk to Kimmage. Feeling guilty, we'd stop off at Mount Argus Church for confession, and later, clean candle grease from the brass penny candle stands in Our Lady's grotto to make up for the sweets, and 'to help' Grandfather with his church volunteer work. We'd arrive in Granny's around noon. Granny, Grandfather and Aunt Ollie, were always happy to see us, there was lots of chat and fun, as they fussed about us.

In winter, Granny always gave us beef stew with curry powder when we arrived. This was because Grandfather was once a British soldier and liked the taste of Indian curry powder. Afterwards, they'd make up the money for us kids to go to the cowboy Western matinee at the Kenilworth Cinema. In summer we kids played in Harold's Cross playground or sometimes in Mount Jerome Cemetery. Summer tea was always salad, picked from the back garden. Memories of warm, freshly boiled, red balls of beetroot were eaten with our fingers and the red juice dyed our hands and face. Scallions were cut into green straws and we sucked our tea through them. After tea, we were given pocket money and it was time to go home. We'd jump backwards off the open bus platform and run to the Banba shop, for a comic, or sweets. Arriving home jaded tired, we were happy and looking forward to next Saturday.

Granny's Beef Stew with Indian Curry Powder

Ingredients: (serves 6)

6 large carrots

2 Spanish onions

1 celery stick

1 large leek

1lb lean stewing beef

2 marrow bones

24 medium size potatoes (flowery variety)

1 tablespoon of Indian curry powder

3 Oxo stock cubes

1 pint cold water.

salt & pepper

Method:

Peel and wash potatoes and set aside, covered in cold water. Peel, wash and chop onions, carrots, celery, and leek. Place the chopped vegetables in a large stock pot. Add stewing beef and marrow bones. Add 1 pint cold water. Sprinkle in Oxo cubes and Indian curry powder. Season with salt and pepper. Place on top of cooker and bring to the boil.

Reduce heat to low gas or 2 electric setting. Allow stew to cook slowly for 2 hours and stir regularly to avoid sticking to pot. Drain water off potatoes and add to stew. Cook for a further 1 hour and continue to stir regularly to avoid sticking. Serve hot with crusty bread.

In Praise of Apples

Dympna Murray Fennell

Ah for the apple, the oldest fruit in the world; it was there in the Garden of Eden – isn't that where Adam got his apple? It's also the most versatile. You can core it, roast it, spice it, dunk it, jelly it, even shoot it, if you can aim like William Tell. If you are the experimental type, you can try the Newton gravity test under your favourite apple tree.

You can also strudel it, at least the Konditoreien in Vienna can, magnificently, wrapping it in delicate filo pastry and flavouring with aromatic spices: the most heavenly treat to be enjoyed in one of the historic coffee houses near the Hofburg – aah!

A far cry from my granny's applecake, done in her bastable oven on the open fire, with red-hot embers cooking the succulent layers within and caramelising the juice that oozed around the edges, and trickled through the crevices in the dough – aaah! The apples came from her own small orchard, and the cloves she used for flavouring came from Zanzibar, halfway around the world. Not that she pondered this bizarre culinary combination, the cloves were an additive to the odd hot whisky which she took for her wheezing chest on cold winter nights.

Nothing was wasted in Granny's apple world. The small wild crabs from the hedgerows were gathered to be made into jelly; a cumbersome business involving jelly bags suspended from upended chairs and dripping the juices through the night; next day there was much boiling and testing until the right gel was reached. The finished produce, with just the right trace of cloves, sweetened many a home-made scone and slice of brown bread in those self-sufficient days.

Granny was selective about her apples and wary of some specimens. She wagged a warning finger about 'rotten apples' that would destroy the whole barrel, as she tried to influence our choice of friends...In this she was not always successful; as Mark Twain said about Adam taking the apple – 2he was only human, he did not want the apple for the apple's sake, he wanted it only because it was forbidden". Granny would not have entertained that kind of permissive philosophy.

I doubt if she would have welcomed Wandering Aengus with his wish 'to pluck 'till time and times are done, the silver apples of the moon, the golden apples of the sun'. Metaphors and poetic language were beyond her – apples were cookers or eaters, Bramley or Pippins. Poet or not, those wandering Aengus types were seldom up to any good. As for the Greek beauty contest over the Apple of Discord for the fairest of the goddesses, that caused almost as much trouble as Adam's taking the forbidden fruit in Eden.

The apple is the universal fruit in all cultures and mythologies, tempting, asking to be plucked, inviting caresses, shaped to be bitten into, lovingly portrayed in still-life paintings, or in comely hands in classic art. As for the Big Apple, there's a whole new world waiting to be explored....

Mushrooming

Joan O'Flynn

Memory can be so unfair. It rejects the ordinary, the mundane, the essential tedium of everyday nurturing. Self-sacrifice goes unnoticed. Larger-than-life colourful expressions of grandeur become wonderful expressions of love. The uncle who called, red-faced and slurring, after the races and threw you a half-a-crown to spend on sweets becomes a hero forever in your mind although intervening years had revealed that his own children rarely got a proper dinner because of his propensity to gamble any few bob he could lay his hands on. The teacher who shouted and swished her cane at your legs and hands can be recalled at will but the gentle lady who coaxed a love of English into your heart remains a shadow. The disgrace of being singled out for ridicule surpasses the joy of winning a prize.

Memory is selective in other ways too. I rarely, for instance, remember my sister being around when I recall my childhood. She must have been there – she is three years older - but she doesn't figure in any of my recall of exploits or adventures. Is that a Freudian lapse or just a woeful admission of self-absorption? Who knows why memory picks and chooses in this way.

My mother was the person who managed the money in our house, making ends meet. My father happily handed over nearly all of his wages to her; cash had a habit of slipping through his fingers. He always bought the first (and dearest) tomatoes of the year, cream cakes on Friday nights, and he liked to speculate on the gee-gees now and again. He was carefree and even-tempered. She was more serious, thoughtful. While remembering my mother conjures up feelings of warmth and security, wisdom and honour, the memories I have of actual outings or adventure belong with my father. Did he enjoy my company or was he delegated to keep a chatter-box of a child out of the way now and again to give my poor mother a break? Whichever is the truth, I have wonderful memories of going to the races on the cross-bar of his bicycle; following the Lily Whites to football fields all over Leinster, even to Croke Park; walking on Sunday at Punchestown before the April meeting; helping to tend the garden, growing my own heads of green lettuce and long orange carrots and picking tiny white new potatoes from brown drills of earth.

My father had learned to cook when he was in the Scouts. He could make stew and produce a tasty fry of rashers and sausages for tea. And he was a great man for cooking mushrooms. A regular treat during the summer was preceded by going through a place we called The Limekiln. This was a disused lime quarry I suspect, fenced off with barbed wire, beside fields that bordered on Naas Race Course. It was there that wonderful flat brown mushrooms could be found. Timing was all-important. You had to be there just before dark or at first light because, my father explained, mushrooms, like fairy toadstools, popped out of the ground suddenly, silently and secretly at those times.

Once you arrived at your destination, you had to equip yourself with a strong piece of grass graced with an appropriately fulsome fluffy top. Then, in the faltering light, you searched the ground beneath your feet for the elusive fungus which was plucked with great care from the earth, making sure to keep the velvety cap intact. With even greater delicacy the grass was threaded through the stalk so that it could be safely carried. As soon as we had a grass-full for each hand we would head for home, negotiating the dreaded barbed wire even more gingerly than on the outward journey, as we held our treasures away from the rusty projectiles that threatened our clothes and our limbs.

And then home to peel and cut up our harvest and cook them for supper. I can still see the toast browning on the long fork before the reddened bars of the range and smell the saucepan on the hob as the milk changed colour, becoming creamier, browner until our supper was ready.

Why is it that this simple supper repast comes to mind when I recall my childhood, while the flavour of the breakfasts, dinners and teas prepared by my mother has dimmed over the years? Is it because it conjures up the one-to-one relationship that was so special, and the feeling of interdependency that accompanies it? Or is it that my father's birthday was last week – he would have been 108 years old. Sadly he didn't live long enough to see his grand-children mushrooming. He would have loved that.

To Stew Mushrooms:

Cut mushrooms into halves or quarters and place in medium sized saucepan. Cover with milk. Add pepper and salt and a good knob of butter. Simmer for about 20 minutes until tender. Thicken the sauce with 1 dessertspoonful of cornflower blended with milk.

Serve on well-buttered toast.

Dad's Dublin Coddle

Leonard Gibbons

My father was born in Dublin's city centre in the area that is known as The Liberties, "a stone's throw" away from Dublin Castle.

Dad was a gentle, quiet and dignified man, well respected by all who knew him. He was a loving father who worked hard all his life and made many sacrifices for the good of our family. He was a religious man who never smoked or gambled, he liked a pint of Guinness and that may be the pointer to the only 'crime' of self-indulgence he could be found guilty of.

He was the first to get up each morning of the week and would have a hot bowl of porridge on the table ready for us children each morning of our schooldays. On Sundays he would prepare breakfast for all the family. It would be a full Irish, rashers sausages, eggs with black/white pudding and fried bread. But for himself he'd make a white Dublin coddle. He would prepare it before he cooked our breakfast and apply the finishing touches when he had served us our meal.

Dad would then sit down besides us and tuck into his coddle, using his knife and fork, slicing up his rashers and sausages and adding a portion of onion to each mouthful with some of the broth dripping off his fork back onto the plate, never wasting a morsel. When his plate was near empty save for the broth he would then call upon his slices of buttered bread and like Leopold Bloom and his cat, he would lap up the white creamy broth until he had cleaned off his plate. Satisfied he would then lean back in his chair with a contented smile on his face, ready to meet the day.

We accepted his quaint tradition without ever uttering a word. As we grew older we linked the coddle to his weekly trip to the local pub. It was religion that gave him away in the end. Each night you see, before bedtime, we would kneel together and say the family rosary. However on Saturday afternoons Dad would go to the pub and have a few pints of Guinness with his brothers. He would arrive home with a grin the size of James's Gate on his face at about 7 pm and by the time we got round to saying our rosary he'd be a bit giddy. He would get his decades and stations mixed up and it would not be long before we'd all end up in fits of giggles around the bed. Dad was a happy drinker and would see the funny side of his predicament; at that stage he would adjourn prayers which was okay by us. When we were old enough to guess that the coddle was his 'hair of the dog' to settle his tummy, he left us in charge of saving our own souls. That memory has stayed with us ever since and is mentioned at all our family gatherings whenever our little clan celebrates a birth, marriage or death.

Dad was in his eighty-fifth year when he passed away following a short illness in 2007. He passed away as he had lived quiet and dignified, to the last.

Dad's Dublin Coddle

Preparation time: 5 minutes

Cooking Time: 30/35 minutes

Serves: 1 person

Ingredients:

2 back or collar rashers

2 pork sausages

1 medium sliced onion

1 pint of water

¼ pint of milk

salt & pepper

1-3 spoonfuls of corn flour

Optional: 2 slices of buttered bread

Method:

Pour one pint of water into a small saucepan. Add in sausages and rashers. Slice onion and add in. Season with a sprinkle of salt and pepper. Bring up to boil and then simmer for 30/35 minutes until your 'happy' meat is well cooked and onions are soft. Mix corn flour with cold milk before adding to saucepan. The more corn flour you add, the thicker the coddle. Stir in well and then allow to stand for two minutes before serving on a piping hot plate.

Fried Rice, Nigerian Style

Ashabi Fafunwa

I am from Nigeria, and my tribe is Yoruba. This tribe is mostly to be found in Southwest Nigeria and Benin. The Yoruba is famous for art and craft. It is also believed that the first descendent of the Yoruba, the Odudua, came from Egypt.

At the moment I live in Ireland, Dublin, Killinarden Apartments. I have two children Arinola and Bisoye and they are both girls. I am always busy because one of my little girls, she is two and a half years and the other is ten months. I like to cook for my family every weekend. My favourite food is fried rice and I will explain how to prepare and cook fried rice.

Preparation:

First of all you need to have meat or chicken. When the meat is cooked add salt. Fry rice and boiled meat/chicken together using olive oil or any cooking oil, add onions, add curry power, pepper, some vegetable (like carrots). Sometimes I add prawns and then I add water and leave it to boil and get well cooked. I will leave it on the stove for 20 minutes. Being Nigerian, I love to have hot food with very hot pepper and not only for me but even my children. They too eat that hot pepper. Then I serve my family. I know my family like it because they always ask me for the same food.

Flavours of Home

Family Memory

_____

_____

_____

_____

_____

_____

_____

_____

_____

_____

_____

_____

_____

Iseloge!

Vanessa Ogida

Iselogbe! Ogbe sena! Those were the words in the air as everyone woke up that day to a nice, bright sunny morning, the first of January 1990- the dawn of another New Year's day in my home town. I am from Edo State in Nigeria, West Africa. Edot State is in the Southern part of Nigeria. Daddy, Mummy, Grandma, Uncles, Aunties and some of my many siblings were already downstairs, around the fire- place, where the yam was to be roasted.

It was a tradition in the house to roast a tuber of yam on every first day of the year and share it amongst everyone- this to my family at the time signified togetherness, sharing and caring for one another. It was also a tradition then to have a bath on that day as soon as you woke up - this also signified entering the New Year in total cleanliness.

Grandma, being the eldest member of my extended family at the time, started with a prayer to the ancestors which was her own belief. Dad followed with his prayer which was neither here nor there. This was because he never gave fully to Christianity or to the traditional way of worship. I will prefer to refer to him then, as somewhere in the middle. My mum and step-mothers also had their chance to pray.

My mum was a strong Catholic at the time and she prayed in the very traditional, Catholic way. My step-mothers prayed in their Anglican and Protestant ways respectively.

A chosen tuber of yam from the yam barn, by my father, was again presented to the ancestors. After this, it was placed in the fire to roast. Everyone waited excitingly and patiently for the yam to roast. Once roasted, it was cut into many pieces to go round the many members of the extended family and then served with palm oil seasoned with salt to taste.

Yam and Palm Oil Meal

Ingredients:
one tuber of yam
500ml palm oil
salt to taste

Method:
Set an open fire. Put a wire gauze over it. Place tuber of yam on the wire gauze, turning it repeatedly as it is roasting. Keep turning until yam's back is completely roasted. Cut into halves to see if the inside is cooked thoroughly. Cut into pieces and serve.

Flavours of Home

Family Memory

_____

_____

_____

_____

_____

_____

_____

_____

_____

_____

_____

_____

_____

_____

Sunday Roast

Bernadette Day

Sundays are a day apart. For our family, the routine was 11 o'clock Mass, after which we would watch TV while my parents cooked the big dinner. Roast beef, roast and mash potatoes, carrots, garden peas and rich gravy made from the juices of the meat. Mam and Dad worked well together: quiet and efficient, peeling, chopping, basting, then a quick read of the Sunday papers to a soundtrack of bubbling and hissing. As Mam deftly plated up steaming hot dinners, dad would bellow "Dinner's ready".

One particular Sunday, because my older brother was on duty in the barracks, there was just eight of us 'round the table. Dinner was usually quiet, we were a bit young for engaging conversation, but there was the odd interjection of "sit up straight" and "keep your elbows down". Dessert was a grand affair: fruit cocktail, crushed meringues, dream topping, covered with flaked chocolate. Straight after the meal Mam disappeared into the sitting room with her black tea and the newspapers tucked under her arm. Dad organised us older children into clearing, washing and sweeping. When my bit was done, as was my habit, I took myself to my pal across the road to gossip over last night's doings at the 'Oasis', the local school disco.

Coming home after our girlish gigglings, I saw there was a military green van parked outside our garden wall. As soon as I opened the front door I could hear Mam wailing and – blood chillingly - Dad roaring crying. Never in my fifteen years had I heard my father crying. I stood outside the kitchen door to listen but I couldn't make out a coherent sentence and so I went into the back room, laid my head on the homework desk and cried silently. I didn't know why I was crying – I think because my strong, unflappable Dad was. An eternal half-hour later, my father looked in at me through the open door, a man twenty years older than the one who had rallied the post-dinner troops. I gathered with my younger brothers and sisters in the sitting room, frightened. Voice and heart breaking, Mam told us that our big brother was dead. Misadventure with a gun while on guard duty. The air immediately filled with childish lamenting. My youngest sister, not yet two, toddled between us, bewildered, crying, not knowing why, but she knew to join in.

Some Sundays later, the potatoes burned and the stench of scorched pot filled the house. Mam and Dad swept us into the car and we drove out to Howth. A hotel dinner was only for State days and Holy Communions – the cost of treating a large family was quite prohibitive, but grief knows no expense. To my teenage mortification, Mam told the waitress why we were there and we got wonderful and teary-eyed, service. The following Sunday, normal service was resumed. The remaining children shuffled up to bridge the gap, and the younger ones ate hungrily, passing peas and roast potatoes on to those who preferred them but retorts about table manners stuck in Mam's throat along with the beef.

It took many years for Sundays to become less strained and one by one we left our places at the dinner table. Then Mam and Dad could easier afford to take the youngest siblings out for a Sunday carvery. But roast beef will always taste of grief.

Tolstoy's Baby

Martha Giblin

Yesterday, we sat in a restaurant in a small village called Tarmonbarry which straddles the counties of Longford and Roscommon, raising a glass of Argentinean red wine. As we tucked into our Thai beef salad, we looked over at our blonde, blue eyed son sitting proudly in his high chair. A year to the day, we had brought this beautiful baby boy home to Ireland from Russia, to be raised in our home in Clondalkin in South Dublin County.

Twelve months ago, we travelled north towards Moscow from a town called Tula, where Leo Vladimir was born. Naturally, the flight home was at six am which meant serious sleep deprivation for one and all. Arising at three am to make the airport in plenty of time, little Leo who was still in the clutches of sleep, had to be carried from the cot in the hotel room to the awaiting taxi. It felt like we were stealing out of the city under the cover of darkness. Gingerly carrying our porcelain doll, we said farewell to a city so large in scale, that it made Manhattan look like…..well, Tarmonbarry.

Our first visit to Russia had occurred three months previously when we travelled to Tula to visit the orphanage where little Leo was living. As we sat on a garden bench positioned in the shade waiting for the staff to bring him out, I sat motionless as if I was having an out of body experience. It had taken us four and a half years to get to this day and I recall spending the whole morning trying to suppress tears. Applying make up at the dressing table in the hotel room, attempting to cover the puffiness of four hours sleep, I asked myself, "if this is the happiest day of my life, why do I feel so wretched? " My husband, Kevin had warned me not to cry. He reckoned that the child would be stressed enough with meeting two strangers who were speaking a different language and that my blubbering like a fool wouldn't help matters…….

The day before we met little Leo, we travelled a few miles outside the city to visit the country estate of Leo Tolstoy. Trying to act like tourists, we attempted to quell our nerves. We learned that he was an advocate for children and had set up a village school to educate the children of the local peasants. Seeing the desk where he had written *Anna Karenina* was amazing. What was more amazing was the fact that his enormous portrait was located on the wall of the majestic hall leading to the courtroom where the local judge presided over our application to formally adopt Leo. Our new Russian son had been christened Vladimir by his birth mother. It was our wish to christen him Leo after my husband's late father, keeping Vladimir as his middle name.

Back at the orphanage which was located on Leo Tolstoy Street, the moment had arrived when a little baby with a pale complexion, in a blue babygro, was handed to us. He sat incredulously looking at both of us not quite sure who we were or what we were doing there. He looked so delicate, we were almost afraid to touch him lest he might break. Our hearts were bursting with joy as the pain in my throat from suppressing my tears subsided. Little did we think as we sat in the stifling heat of that day that we would be sitting around a snug table at a restaurant in Tarmonbarry one year on, cutting up ham, cabbage and potatoes washed down with watery Mi Wadi in the company of his doting Co. Longford Granny. It's just what our baby loves....Tolstoy would have approved.

Keeping the Juices Flowing

Mary Mylod Okafo

Smells of childhood. Tastes of young adulthood. And later, a hectic working life. If I was to list the memories that excited my senses most, there would be a long list. But some. When as a young child, sitting at my grandmother's table, the waft of warm milk straight from the cow. Or salty butter, freshly made. And me, in the cold corner of the parlour, mashing it through my fingers before it slid down my throat. All done silently for fear of being caught.

Coddle, in my mother's kitchen in Ballyfermot on Saturday, mine had to have Bisto in it because it looked like frothy water without it, but the salty taste clings to my lips still. Creamy rice pudding, with sultanas on a Friday night after dinner, of battered fish and mother's homemade chips. Well, it was Friday, wasn't it?!

But for my own young family, the tastes were of a different place. A man who hailed from a far away land where heat and colour were the order of the day. This was where our boys took their taste buds from. Red pepper, cayenne, for heat. Great for a cold to clear the sinuses. Peanut butter to thicken, this was the nearest Ireland could come to the original in the 1970's. Tomatoes pureed and chillies for colour. Curry powder to scent the air and stimulate the juices. All things new in a time of change.

Arriving in Dublin in a Maxwell House jar, via London, by way of some family member or visitor from Africa. And ground rice. Grainy and starchy. To help shovel the stew into a waiting gob. No need for a spoon, that would just spoil the taste. No Asian market then. No Parnell Street and Moore Street was still all "apples and oranges" and "get your bananas here". And the smells, the heat and the taste would stick to the wallpaper as well as to the hairs in your nose and stay with you for days. On your lips you could taste it forever.

Even as I put these words on paper, I can smell it in the air, a bouquet of memories for the palette.

Flavours of Home

Family Recipe

_____

_____

_____

_____

_____

_____

_____

_____

_____

_____

_____

_____

_____

Pink Icing

Veronica O'Neill

Ireland was a greener state of mind when I was growing up. Leaner. Naive. Big families were the norm then, a must do, must have. More duty than choice. Decreed by a power that held much sway at that time. With a God and the devil over-riding every detail, baked together in a pie, threatening, in constant battle for our soul, good old fear helped a people oblige.

There were nine of us altogether in a brood, leaving very little room to wriggle. A living then was more thinly sliced. A home-maker had to be creative, inventive, an all-rounder. Juggle finances, become proficient in economics. Making a little stretch further seemed a minor miracle. Miracles happened often. No such thing then as waste. Wanton. Sinful. Waste not, want not became the mantra. Food not in the first flush of youth but had not as yet crossed over was put to good use. Made into another dish. Soft tomatoes found themselves in sauces, stews, casseroles. Over-ripe fruit became jam, chutney. Stale bread became bread and butter pudding, was fried, made into croutons. Day old or more than a day old boiled potatoes were made into potato cakes or farls. Tasted great, hot, straight from the pan smothered in real butter.

Gur cake, my favourite, was yet another use of stale bread. "Flies graveyard" some used to call it. Thankfully, though, as far as I know, no dead were ever sighted or reported buried in our mix. Just fruit plumped and swelled by an over-night stay in tea together with brown sugar, bread cut in small pieces, crusts removed and a little grate of lemon rind. Next day, sieved flour and beaten eggs were added to the fruity mixture. Well rested pastry, made from scratch, was cut in half, rolled out onto a floured table, making a top and base for to house the mixture. A tin was greased and lined with the pastry, bottom and sides, the fruit mixture generously spooned, pastry on top and the picture was nearly complete. Just a trim and a pinch around the edges to make it tidy and decorative. Then into the oven for about thirty minutes or until golden brown. Smelled like Christmas pudding. Tasted heavenly. Then out to cool before pink icing, yes, always pink icing was smoothed on top. Cut then into squares, proudly and carefully set on a large plate with a doily. Never did it last long though. All too soon it was gone and after all that effort. Good comfort food though. Slow cooking, fast eating.

Flavours of Home

Family Memory

_____

_____

_____

_____

_____

_____

_____

_____

_____

_____

_____

_____

_____

Molly's Kitchen

Shirley Anne Plunkett

One of the highlights of my childhood was the wonderful smells wafting from Grandmother Molly's kitchen. Her specialty was meat dishes, simple natural food. Irish stew made with lamb or beef was one of my favourites as was Shepard's Pie. It was fun to watch the beef being pressed through the holes of her mincing machine. Her gentle hands shaped it with diced onion, egg and flour to make rissoles/beef burgers. Molly was from Kerry and tragically her mother died in childbirth. When her father remarried, Molly and her siblings were sent away to different relatives. Growing up without a loving family must have been very hard and Molly ran away to Dublin at the age of 16 to work for wealthy people as a maid.

Eventually, she married a much older Welsh man and had three children. Her husband was an angry man who died when my Mother was 12 years old. For a woman who had very little love in her life, Nana put a lot of love into her food and cooking for those she loved. Every Saturday evening when Mum, my brother and I visited, her frying pan sizzled with rashers, sausages and black and white pudding and not to forget, tasty fried bread. She didn't use recipes; she just had a cook's knowing.

My other grandmother's specialty was homemade apple tart. Every Sunday we visited she made a salad with home cooked ham or corned beef and thinly sliced onions in vinegar which my brother and I loved but have never eaten since.

Every Friday, Mother received fresh fish and on occasion fresh shrimp courtesy of Grandfather directly from the Dublin fish market where he worked. The cod or whiting was delicious and was always served fried with handmade chips. On cold winter nights I remember holding slices of white bread over the fire's hot coals on a long fork and we ate the toast for supper with lashings of butter.

Today my favourite food is homemade and hopefully I can share the love of good food with my son and future generations.

Flavours of Home

Family Recipe

From the Celestial Table

Triona Walsh

I didn't realise when I was a child how lucky I was. Most summers my parents were able to afford to take us away on holidays, generally to France. But did I really appreciate it then? Not at all. I guess I thought every child got to go to France every summer and eat orange cantaloupe and salty Parma ham in the balmy Brittany sunshine.

And I'm afraid I actively didn't like some parts of the experience. I got car sick, sea sick and my aversion to the hole in the ground toilets at motorway stops forged a bladder of steel. But one year the travelling was particularly trying, when we went further afield. My father, a talented violinist, had a group of musician friends in Switzerland. So, we drove further into the continent to spend three weeks with them. But, oh the struggle to get there. We drove across Europe in a red Audi, and somewhere on the soulless autobahn, the engine broke. I'm sure there was a more technical explanation, but as far as I understood, the engine just broke.

But we got there. A tow truck, a rescue from our friend Hans Pater, and we finally arrived in stunning St Gallen, in the east of Switzerland. It was here that I first tasted pasta. I was seven years old and I'd never tasted anything as delicious. Hans Pater's wife, Marianne, served it to us outside on their terrace, under the shade of vine leaves. I later snuck into the kitchen and sank little hands into the bowl of left over pasta shells and shoved as many handfuls of this exquisite new food into my mouth. But if I thought that was heaven, it was merely a glorious appetizer. My sheltered palate was wonderfully assaulted with new tastes left, right and centre. Though I drew the line at the pink pickled squid that was served up at one holiday barbeque.

The pinnacle of the culinary journey that I went on that year in Switzerland, was reached quite literally at the pinnacle of one of the many Swiss alps. I am quite sure it was one of the smaller ones; otherwise I doubt they would have built a restaurant at the top of it! But it was still freezing, and the glare from the July snow has forever bathed this memory in a sort of beatific glow. Placed in front of us children were plates of rösti. And perhaps it was because we were so close to God, high up in the mountains, touching the azure sky, that it tasted like crumbs dropped from the celestial table. It was so simple, potato, grated, cooked in butter... but it wasn't that simple. It was the size of the small grated potato pieces, or maybe it was the amount of butter. Perhaps it was just the right amount of salt added. But whatever it was, everyone adored it. As all holidays do, it came to an end and we retraced our steps back across the European motorways, thankfully this time without the breakdown drama.

Unlike the trips to France which sometimes merged into one another in our memories, this trip to Switzerland stayed crisp and fresh. We tried our hand at making rösti when we were home. And it was nice, but it never compared to that mountain top feast. Now, thirty years on from the trip this dish is still spoken of in reverent tones at home. We've all got families of our own (who are being brought to France *and* reminded of how lucky they are.) We've got busy lives and don't see each other as much as we would like. But a short cut to our bond, to remembrance of times past, is that one word rösti. Ahhhhhhhhh.

Ingredients: (for 4 people)

1 kg raw potatoes, 1 tablespoon salt, 3-4 tablespoons butter.

Method:

Peel the potatoes and use the rösti grater to grate them into fine strips. Get the potato as dry as possible with kitchen paper. Heat the butter in the frying pan. Add the potatoes, sprinkle with salt and stir well to mix them in with the butter. Cover and fry for 20-30 minutes over medium heat, turning regularly. Then uncover the pan, turn the heat up and fry for a further 20 minutes. Do not stir!

Aggie's Apple Tarts

Derek Finn and Maria Finn

The centre of our childhood week was Saturday. It was Saturday when the turf- boys came with thick plastic bags stacked with sods. It was Saturday when the fruit and veg. van came with the potatoes and cabbage and cooking apples. It was Saturday when my mother would wheel out the twin-tub washing machine with the hand wringer and tackle the week's laundry. It was Saturday when the stew was cooked for dinner and the sausages fried for tea. Above all, it was Saturday when my mother would work her weekly magic and produce the best apple tarts in Ireland.

On Saturday mornings my mother's ever clean kitchen descended into an unholy clutter of children and washing machines and tables and television. The kitchen was the centre of our house, and the centre of the kitchen was the range, the four-footed solid fuel stove that warmed our feet, cooked our food, and heated our water. In a house without central heating the kitchen doubled as dining room, living room, and laundry room. My mother would drag the washing machine from its hiding place and into the middle of the floor and set to work. She loaded the first batch of laundry and started on the stew to come and piled the apples on the table for the tart to follow. The stew held little interest for us; we were turned off by the raw potatoes and red meat and tuned in instead to the television blaring in the corner. Only when the mixing bowl was pulled down from the cupboard did we get up and shuffle over, smiling and sort-of-willing to help.

Ignoring the hungry eyes my mother mixed the flour, water, egg and butter in the bowl, kneading the pastry mixture with her fingers into a white lump that looked like play dough. She dusted the table with fine flour and began to flatten and roll the pastry to fit the dinner plate that would act as a baking pan. My mother never used a rolling- pin, she always used an empty glass milk bottle, plucked from its spot on the doorstep. Once the pastry was ready it was time to add the apples. We were thrown an apple or two and told to peel the skin. In the time it took us to hack away at our apples, my mother would have peeled several pounds of big cookers. We would always wonder at her agility with a peeling knife, running it over apple after apple, the skin descending like a winding staircase. Her skill was such that we could take the peeled, continuous skin and reconstruct a hollow apple. We never knew what type of apple was used, all we knew was that they were cooking apples and the skins tasted very tart, so much so that we generously dipped them in sugar, sometimes we would lick the sugar off and double dip the sticky skin. This was our favourite part of the morning, this was our favourite part of the week. Meanwhile my mother sliced and arrayed the apples in the pastry sandwich, skimmed the overhanging top layer, and sealed the edges with the prongs of a dinner fork. She repeated this with two or three tarts, shoving each into the oven in the range, the temperature gauge on the outside firmly in the red.

In the next hour or so my mother would finish up the laundry, set the stew to simmer on top of the range, and restore the kitchen to its previous state of hygienic grace. The smell of oxtail soup from the stew mingled with the sweet aroma of baking apples and pastry. In time the tarts were removed and allowed to cool, steaming and crisp in the corner of the kitchen. The next we saw of them was after dinner, when they were sliced and served as dessert. To us children the apple tarts made by our aunts and grandfather (the army cook) were very foreign, full as they were of spicy cloves and glazed on the outside with jagged shards of baked sugar. We loved our mother's simple apple tarts; the cooked apples were soft and tangy, the pastry crisp, with a dryness that called for a cup of strong tea. On Sundays we were allowed to have custard or even ice- cream with our tart. By Monday the once full dinner plates were reduced to crumbs, the apple tarts were gone and we were left again to wait for Saturday.

Aggie's Apple Tart

Ingredients:

1lb plain flour

pinch of salt

10 – 12 oz margarine

2 egg yolks

2 tsp of caster sugar

4 large cooking apples

Water to mix

Method:

Sieve the flour and salt together. Cut the margarine into small pieces, rub it lightly into the flour, using the finger tips. Add the sugar, mix to a stiff paste with the egg yolks and one tablespoon of water. Use more water if necessary. Roll out the pastry and place on a plate. Peel, slice apples and place in saucepan and cover with a small amount of water. When the apples are partially cooked, put on plate and sprinkle with sugar. Cover with remainder of pastry. Pre-heat oven. Cooking time approximately 45 minutes, gas mark 6 or 200 F.